To Granny,

Love

C000282773

Making
AUSTRALIAN
WILDFLOWERS
For
Cake Decorating

Making
AUSTRALIAN
WILDFLOWERS
For
CAKE DECORATING

SUE OTERI

DOROTHY PARSONS

HUTCHINSON AUSTRALIA

Created and produced by
Emerald Hill House and
The Bookmakers Group Pty. Ltd.
for
Century Hutchinson Australia Pty. Ltd.
20 Alfred Street, Milsons Point NSW 2061

Sydney Melbourne London
Auckland Johannesburg
and agencies throughout the world

First Published 1989

© Sue Oteri and Dorothy Parsons 1989
© Photographs: Emerald Hill House

National Library of Australia
Cataloguing-in-publication data

All rights reserved. No part of this publication
may be reproduced, stored in a retrieval system,
or transmitted in any form or by an means,
electronic, mechanical, photocopying, recording
or otherwise, without the prior permission of
the Publisher.

National Library of Australia
Cataloguing-in-Publication Data

Oteri, Sue.
    Making Australian wildflowers for cake decorating.

    ISBN 0 09 169480 9.

    1. Cake decorating. 2. Sugar art. 3. Wild
    flowers — Australia. I. Parsons, Dorothy.
    II. Title.

641.8'653

Printed in Hong Kong
Typeset in 11/12pt Garamond by The Type Shop, New South Wales

Editor: Celia Tikotin
Art Editor: Alan Fisher
Photography: David Liddle • Gary Chowanetz
Calligraphy: Kathleen Phelps
Designed by Alan Fisher

AUSTRALIA CAKE

Each State flower is combined with the national flower (Wattle) to make this colourful and attractive spray: New South Wales — Waratah, Queensland — Cooktown Orchid, Victoria — Pink Heath, Western Australia — Kangaroo Paw, Northern Territory — Sturt's Desert Rose, Australian Capital Territory — Alpine Bluebell, South Australia — Sturt's Desert Pea, Tasmania — Blue Gum.

Contents

Contents

Welcome to cake decorating with Australian wildflowers!

We have given you two photos of each flower. There is a step-by-step photo, which starts at the top left and finishes at the bottom right. There is also a photo of the completed flower. Use it as a guide to colouring and assembling your work.

Sue Oteri

Dorothy Parsons

Materials

Notes on Materials

1 Chalks used for colouring flowers **must always be non toxic.**

2 There are many recipes for modelling paste and cake decorators all have their favourite. Here is ours.

Ingredients
200 g pure icing sugar
2 level teaspoons gelatine (use a 4ml teaspoon)
2 rounded teaspoons liquid glucose
28 ml water.

Method
Sprinkle gelatine over water in a small glass or china bowl and allow to become spongy. Dissolve over gentle heat. Add glucose when dissolved and mix well. Sift icing sugar into china or glass bowl. Make a well in the centre, pour in the clear liquid and stir until thoroughly combined. Store in a plastic airtight container at room temperature. Allow to stand overnight before use.

To use this mixture, take out the amount you require and knead with pure icing sugar until it is a smooth consistency — it should feel like a soft plasticine.

To give flowers a smoother texture, after kneading the paste, add a small amount of plastic icing. The proportion should be about 2 parts paste to 1 part icing.

Some flowers, such as the Golden Everlasting, the Cooktown Orchid and the Sturt's Desert Pea need a paste of firmer consistency. Simply add a little cornflour to your mixture.
Modelling paste is sometimes listed as coloured. You do not buy it this way, but colour it yourself, using a drop or two of liquid food colouring.

Materials

Notes on Materials

3 Stamens come in three sizes: fine, medium and thick.

4 The length of wire used is not crucial — whenever we have not specified a length, we use a piece 5 cm long, because that is a handy length to work with for us — maybe not for you.

5 We use three gauges of wire: fine, medium and thick.

6 The amount of modelling paste used is usually measured by reference to the small, medium and large pinheads. Here are the relevant sizes:

actual size

7 A very fine paintbrush is usually the most suitable for painting the flowers. A makeup brush, because softer, is best for dusting the flowers with chalk.

8 Most of you will have a set of modelling tools, some will not. For simplicity, we have generally referred to substitutes, such as a skewer for veining leaves, but of course, if you have the relevant modelling tool, use it!

9 The number, shapes and names of petal cutters on the market are ever increasing and changing. We refer to the ones we use by name, but a reproduction is given of each cutter used, of exactly the same size and shape, to ensure complete accuracy. If you cannot find one of the cutters, this enables you to trace it on to cardboard, and cut paste from your tracing.

10 Before rolling out your modelling paste always dust your workboard lightly with cornflour.

11 Liquid food colouring is nearly always diluted with spirits. Pure alcohol is best, but expensive.

12 Sometimes we have specified moistening shapes with eggwhite or water to bind them together. Either will do and in fact a mixture of rose water and gum arabic is also very successful. Simply mix 1 part gum arabic to 3 parts rose water and store in an airtight container.

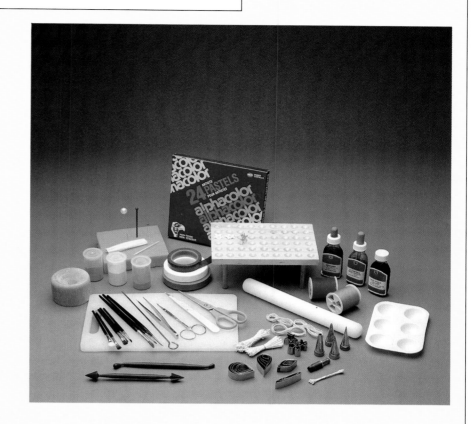

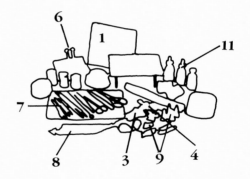

GUMNUT BABY AND ECHIDNA PLAQUE

First prize Royal Melbourne Show 1988.
An outstanding floral arrangement of Yellow Banksia, Flannel Flower, Dagger Wattle and Kangaroo Paw.

Barrier Range Wattle

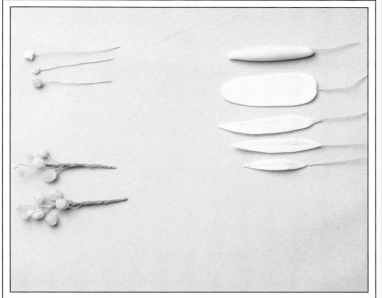

Floral emblem of Australia

Materials

fine wire; royal icing; size 1 piping tube and bag; lemon yellow, egg yellow and leaf green liquid food colouring; water; medium paintbrush; castor sugar; paper towels; eggwhite; leaf green modelling paste; small rolling pin; 8009 B C and D waterlily cutters; pin; skewer; spirits; green parafilm stem wrap

FLOWER

Make *9* small
Make *10* large

Hook wire at one end. Use royal icing mixed to a firm peak consistency. With tube and bag, pipe a ball the size of the small pinhead on top of the hooked wire. Make 9. Allow to dry. Then make 10 more, with a slightly larger ball of icing on each wire. Allow to dry.

To colour the flowers, mix 1 part lemon yellow food colouring with 10 parts water. Paint flowers, dip in castor sugar and allow to dry on paper towels.

LEAF

Make *7*

Insert wire moistened with eggwhite halfway into a ball of leaf green modelling paste the size of the large pinhead. Roll paste into shape shown, then roll out thinly. Use 3 waterlily cutters to cut different sized leaves. Flatten the edges of the leaf with your fingertips. Make a vein down the centre of each leaf with a pin. Dry leaf in the shape you want. For example, lay it lengthwise over a skewer to curve it naturally.

To colour, mix 1 part leaf green and 1 part egg yellow liquid food colouring with 8 parts spirits. Paint the leaves. Allow to dry.

ASSEMBLY

Start with 1 small ball of wattle. Position 2 other small balls just bellow and on either side of the first ball. Repeat with 2 large balls, positioning them below and beween the upper 2 balls. Repeat with remaining large balls. This is a 7 ball spray.

Attach another 7 ball spray to one side of the completed stem, just below the leaves, then add a 5 ball spray on the opposite side. Add one more leaf just below the last spray. For the 5 ball spray, simply do not add the last 2 large balls.

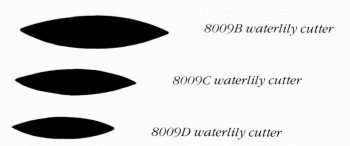

8009B waterlily cutter

8009C waterlily cutter

8009D waterlily cutter

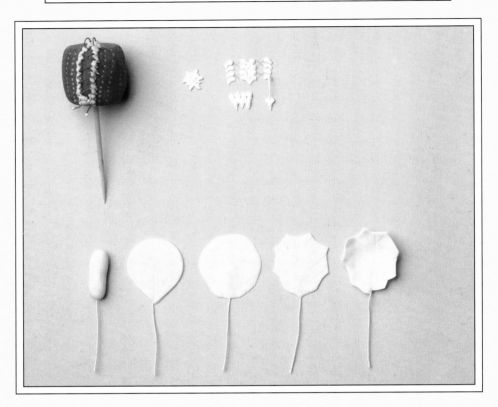

Materials

white and green modelling paste; small rolling pin; cocktail stick; small pin; pillar box red, rose pink, black, sky blue, egg yellow, caramel brown and leaf green liquid food colouring; spirits; medium paintbrush; tweezers; 2 cm lengths fine wire; 2 cm lengths stamens; royal icing; size 1 piping tube and bag; skewer; grey chalk; brush for dusting; 8 cm lengths medium wire; eggwhite; T12 D cutter; scissors

FLOWER

Make 1

Using white modelling paste, roll a barrel shape 3 cm wide and 3 cm long. Flatten the top and the bottom. Insert cocktail stick halfway through the base of the shape. Using a small pin, make a circle of 18 dots, 5 mm in from the edge of the top. Make a line down the sides of the shape by piercing 13 more holes under each of the 18 (making 14 rows in all).

To colour, mix 1 part pillar box red and 2 parts rose pink food colouring with 2 parts spirits and paint the entire flower. Allow to dry thoroughly — for at least a week.

With tweezers, thread one end of fine wire into one top hole and the other end into the hole below, making a loop. Repeat 17 times, looping the top 2 circles of holes. Using the tweezers, thread one end of fine wire in a hole on the third line. Thread a second piece of wire in the hole next to the first

piece of wire. Cross the wire and thread each end into the holes below, on the fourth row. Continue in this manner down the next 8 rows of holes, covering all of the shape except the last 2 rows. Using the tweezers, insert 36 slightly curved stamens into the remaining 2 rows of holes.

Colour peak consistency royal icing with 1 part black and 1 part sky blue food colouring to make a pale blue-grey.

Start from the top of the flower and pipe a teardrop at the base of each loop. Continue piping circles of teardrops until the entire top is covered. Pipe a row of teardrops down one row at base of wires. Repeat on the next row, interlocking teardrops as shown as you pipe. Cover the last 2 rows and underneath the flower with circles of overlapping teardrops. Allow to dry.

To colour, mix 1 part pillar box red and 1 part rose pink liquid food colouring with 2 parts spirits and

Scarlet Banksia

paint the wire and base of stamens (not the tips). Next, mix 1 part egg yellow liquid food colouring with 2 parts spirits and paint the tips of stamens. Allow to dry. Finally, dust grey chalk over the piped area in between the wires.

LEAF
Make 6

Using green modelling paste, roll a sausage shape. Moisten one end of medium wire with eggwhite. Insert moistened end of wire halfway through, then roll flat with rolling pin. Cut flattened shape using the cutter. Flatten further with fingertips. Cut out shape of leaf with scissors. Etch veins with pin as shown. Using pinhead, gently poke between the veins, working from the outer edge to the centre, to curl up the edges and 'dimple' the leaf.

To colour, mix 1 part caramel brown and 2 parts leaf green liquid food colouring with 4 parts spirits and paint the entire leaf. Allow to dry.

ASSEMBLY

Secure 3 leaves at the base of the flower. Secure close to the cocktail stick so no wire will be showing. Secure a further 3 leaves just below and in between the first level of leaves.

T12 D cutter

Brown Boronia

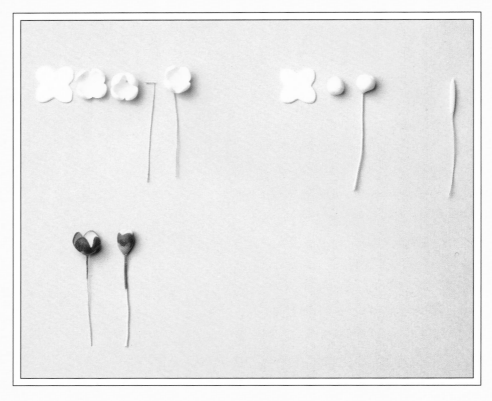

Materials

egg yellow and leaf green modelling paste; small rolling pin; 7098 daphne cutter; airtight container; foam; medium pinhead; small pin; scissors; fine and medium wire; royal icing; rose pink, caramel brown, burgundy and leaf green liquid food colouring; spirits; fine and medium paintbrushes; yellow and light green chalk; brush for dusting; eggwhite; scalpel; brown parafilm stem wrap; size 0 piping tube and bag

FLOWER
Make 7

Roll out egg yellow paste thinly. Cut 10 shapes with cutter. Place each floret in airtight container. Work with a single floret at a time. Place 1 on foam. Using the medium pinhead gently press each petal and then the centre of the floret into the foam. This curves the petal inwards and gives the flower a cupped shape.

Pierce each flower on the base with a small pin. Allow to dry. Using lengths of fine wire, each with a small angled hook on one end, thread three-quarters of the wire through the floret. Add a small amount of flooding consistency royal icing to the centre of the flower, pull wire through. Pipe a dot of icing in the centre to cover the hook. This secures the stem to the flower. Allow to dry. Use the remaining 3 shapes to make buds.

To colour, mix 1 part rose pink, 1 part caramel brown and 1 part burgundy liquid food colouring with 5 parts spirits. Paint the outside of the flowers. Allow to dry. Next, mix 4 parts yellow with 1 part light green chalk and dust the centres. Using a fine paintbrush and the liquid colour mixture, paint a cross in the centre of each flower.

Mix leaf green royal icing to a running consistency. Using the icing and a fine paintbrush, paint a calyx on the base of each flower. Allow to dry. Dust calyx with light green chalk.

 7098 daphne cutter

Brown Boronia

BUD
Make 3

Take 1 shape from the container and roll into a ball. Make a pinhole halfway through the ball. Dip the hooked end of a length of medium wire into eggwhite and insert in pinhole. Pinch the opening closed, to secure the wire. Etch a cross on top of the bud with the scalpel.

To colour, paint the back of buds with the same mixture used on the flowers. Allow to dry. Next, dust the top of the buds with the yellow and green chalk mixture. Paint and colour a calyx on the base of each bud in the same way as you did for the flower.

LEAF
Make 7

Roll a ball of leaf green paste slightly larger than the medium pinhead into a thin cylinder. Moisten one end of a length of fine wire with eggwhite. Insert wire halfway into paste and roll between two fingers and the palm of your hand. Nip off the top and bottom of shape and roll again — this thins out the paste. Repeat until you have a very thin leaf about 1 cm long.

To colour, mix 2 parts leaf green and 1 part caramel brown liquid food colouring with about 8 parts spirits. Paint the leaves using the medium paint-brush. Allow to dry.

ASSEMBLY

Take 3 buds, position at different levels and wrap together with stem wrap. Add flowers and leaves as you trail down the stem. Secure as before.

Yellow Banksia

Materials

white modelling paste; small rolling pin; medium pinhead; cocktail stick; sizes 0 and 1 piping tube and bag; royal icing; stamens; tweezers; yellow, white, cream and lime green chalk; brush for dusting; egg yellow, caramel brown, black and leaf green liquid food colouring; spirits; soft paintbrush; 8 cm lengths medium wire; scissors; corn husk or satay stick; eggwhite; green parafilm stem wrap

FLOWER
Make 1

Roll a large ball of paste approximately 3 cm in diameter. Press the pinhead into the centre of the ball and rotate, to form a hole about 5 cm deep. Slightly flatten the base of the ball, but do not exceed the 3 cm diameter. Insert a cocktail stick into the base of the ball approximately halfway through. This is the stem. Allow to dry thoroughly for about 2 days.

Using size 0 piping tube and peaking consistency royal icing, pipe lines from the inside bottom to the top of the hole. Pipe curved teardrop shapes (shown) around the edge of the hole.

Hold the ball upside down, by holding on to the cocktail stick. Then, using the 'dot and pull' method, pipe a row just under the teardrops. This achieves the effect of small 'tails' protruding from the ball. Continue piping rows using this method

until half the ball is covered. Cover the remainder of the ball using the same method, but make the 'tails' longer and overlapping the previous piped rows in an uneven manner.

As you pipe the longer rows of 'tails', every so often pipe a dot of royal icing. Insert a stamen, cut to 2.5 cm in length with top removed and slightly curved, into this dot, using tweezers. Insert about 35 of these stamens. Cover the entire ball with icing tails. Allow to dry thoroughly.

To colour, dust the longer tails and the base of the flower with yellow chalk. Then mix 1 part cream with 1 part white chalk or cornflour and dust the remainder of the flower and inside the hole.
Mix 1 part egg yellow food colouring with 12 parts spirits and paint stamens with this very pale mixture highlighting the long tails by painting streaks every so often. Carefully paint the tip of each stamen with undiluted caramel brown liquid colouring.

Yellow Banksia

LEAF
Make 5

Using modelling paste, roll a fat sausage shape. Moisten one end of wire and insert it as far as possible without breaking through the top. To ensure the wire is in the centre of the sausage, press outer edges with your fingertips. Flatten with a rolling pin.

Using scissors, cut away the excess on top of the flattened shape, so as the wire sits just below the top of the leaf. Cut the leaf into the irregular shape shown.

Vein the back of the leaf with corn husk, applying enough pressure to leave the horizontal imprint on the leaf. Pinch a prominent centre vein along the length of the back of the leaf with tweezers or, once leaf is dry, pipe a fine line of peaking consistency royal icing with the size 1 tube. Allow leaves to dry in different shapes.

To colour, mix 1 part black and 1 part leaf green liquid food colouring with 12 parts spirits. Paint entire leaf. Allow to dry. Next, mix 1 part lime green with 1 part yellow chalk and dust entire leaf. Paint a fine line of eggwhite down the centre of the back of the leaf. Paint the vein with 1 part egg yellow food colouring mixed with 4 parts spirits.

ASSEMBLY

Position 3 leaves just underneath the flower. Secure with stem wrap. Position a further 2 leaves just below and in between the 3 leaves.

Gumnuts

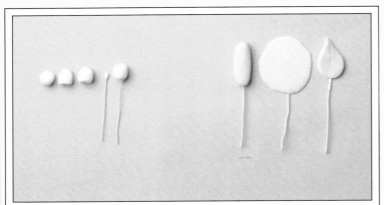

Materials

modelling paste; skewer; small pinhead; foam; fine and medium wire; royal icing; stamens; eggwhite; caramel brown and leaf green liquid food colouring; spirits; paper towels; medium paintbrush; cocoa; small rolling pin; T04 D cutter; pin; skewer; brown parafilm stem wrap

GUMNUT
Make *5*

Dip one end of 5 lengths of fine wire into flooding consistency royal icing to get a small ball on the end wire to make stamens, or just use ready-made stamens. Allow to dry.

Using caramel brown modelling paste (shown as white) make a small pea-sized ball. Insert skewer about three-quarters of the way into the ball, and roll skewered ball backwards and forwards on the palm of your hand — this creates an even hollow in the centre of the ball. Remove skewer and insert small pinhead into hollow. Place ball on foam and roll to get ball back to rounded shape, then roll it on its side to give it a cup shape.

Dip the tip of the stamen into eggwhite. Insert the bottom of the stamen into the hollow of the gumnut and pull it through. Turn the gumnut upside down and press the base of the nut to secure the stamen. Allow to dry in the upside down position.

To colour, mix 1 part caramel brown food colouring with 6 parts spirits. If you are making a large quantity of gumnuts, you may find it easier just to dip each gumnut in the liquid and then drain off the excess by standing gumnuts upside down on paper towels. Otherwise, paint each one. When gumnuts are partly dry, dip them into cocoa. Turn them upside down and allow to dry.

LEAF
Make *1*

Roll paste coloured leaf green into shape shown. Insert moistened end of medium wire halfway and roll out paste thinly. Check that wire is in the centre. Cut leaf with cutter. Flatten the edges of the leaf with your fingertips. Make a vein down the centre of each leaf. Dry leaf in a natural shape, rather than flat, by laying lengthwise over a skewer.

To colour, mix 2 parts leaf green and 1 part caramel brown liquid food colouring with 8 parts spirits and allow to dry.

ASSEMBLY

Using stem wrap, take 1 leaf and 1 gumnut and wrap together. Arrange 4 more gumnuts in a cluster and wrap together.

T04 D cutter

JANINE
This pale green cake features gumnut babies with sprays of Flannel Flowers, Christmas Bells and wattle.
CHRISTENING CAKE
Pink Heath and Astartea Fascicularis add a delicate touch to this cream christening cake.

Pink Boronia

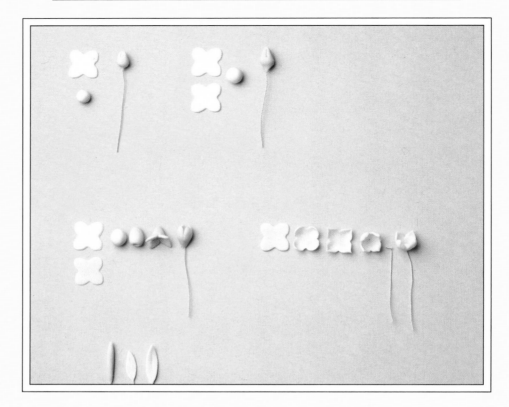

Materials

pale pink and leaf green modelling paste; small rolling pin; 7098 daphne cutter; airtight container; foam; fine wire; eggwhite; scissors; skewer; small and medium pinheads; size 0 piping tube and bag; royal icing; yellow, light green, pink and maroon chalk; twinkle pink dust; cornflour; brush for dusting; leaf green and caramel brown liquid food colouring; spirits; medium paintbrush; green parafilm stem wrap; tweezers

Roll out pale pink paste thinly. Cut 16 florets with the cutter. Place the florets in container. Work with a single floret at a time.

CLOSED BUD
Make *3* small
Make *3* large

For a small bud, make a ball from 1 floret and for a large bud use 2. Moisten the hooked end of wire with eggwhite and insert halfway into ball. Secure wire at base of ball. Mould into teardrop shape. Snip top of bud twice with scissors to make a cross.

OPEN BUD
Make *2*

Take 2 of the florets from the container. Roll into a ball, then shape as shown. Insert a skewer halfway into the thick end of the cone. Using scissors, cut 4 petals on this end. Open petals and pinch the tip of

each petal to create a point on each. Place bud on foam. Press the small pinhead on to the inside of each petal to cup it. Moisten the hooked end of wire with eggwhite. Insert wire through the top centre of bud and pull through. Pinch the base of the bud to secure the wire. Partially close the petals as shown.

FLOWER
Make *3*

Take a floret from the container. Place on foam. Press medium pinhead into centre of each petal. Pinch tip of each petal to a point. Press pinhead into centre of each petal again to cup petals further and in centre of flower. Insert small angled end of wire through the centre of the flower. Using tube and bag, pipe a dot of flooding consistency royal icing into the centre of the flower to conceal the hook of wire. Pierce base of flower with a small pin. Allow to dry.

To colour flowers and buds, first mix equal parts of

Pink Boronia

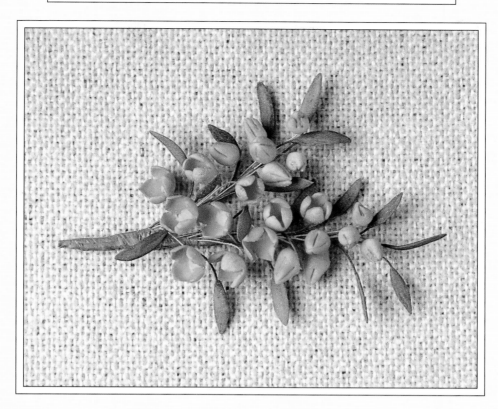

light green and yellow chalk and dust the base of both. Next, mix 2 parts twinkle pink dust, 2 parts pink and 1 part maroon chalk with 1 part cornflour and dust the rest of the flowers and buds. Finally, dust flower centres with yellow chalk.

LEAF
Make 9

Make a ball of leaf green paste slightly larger than the medium pinhead and roll into a long shape. Moisten one end of wire with eggwhite. Insert wire halfway into paste and roll paste between two fingers and the palm of your hand. Nip off the top and bottom of shape, and roll again to thin out the paste. Repeat until you have a thin leaf approximately 1 cm long. Make 4 slightly shorter. Flatten with a rolling pin.

To colour, mix 2 parts leaf green and 1 part caramel brown liquid food colouring with 8 parts spirits. Paint the leaves. Allow to dry.

ASSEMBLY

Position 3 leaves at slightly different levels. Secure with stem wrap. Add 3 small buds just below the leaves. Secure. Position 2 large buds in between and just below small buds. Secure. Place a leaf on either side of them. Secure. Just below, position 2 open buds and 1 large bud at different levels. Add 2 leaves on same level. Secure. Position 3 flowers with 2 leaves on either side and 1 leaf in the middle just below the previous level. Using tweezers, tilt flowers forward to create a drooping effect.

7098 daphne cutter

Golden Everlasting

Materials

*rolling pin; modelling paste; eight petal daisy
cutters; 7 cm lengths fine and medium wire;
eggwhite; egg yellow, lemon yellow, caramel brown
and leaf green liquid food colouring; spirits; fine
and medium paintbrushes; castor sugar; royal
icing; size 1 piping tube and bag; airtight
container; scissors; foam; large and small
pinheads; small brush; 8009 waterlily cutters; small
pin; sky blue, grey and white chalk; brush for
dusting*

FLOWER CENTRE

Make *1*

Roll modelling paste thinly. Cut a shape with the small daisy cutter. Roll into a ball. Hook one end of the wire and bend hook on a rightangle. Moisten hooked end of wire with eggwhite and insert halfway into ball. Pinch the base of the ball to secure the wire. Flatten the top of the ball. Allow to dry.

To colour, mix 2 parts egg yellow and 1 part leaf green colouring with 12 parts spirits to give a lime green colour. Paint the entire centre. Dip in castor sugar and allow to dry. With white royal icing mixed to flooding consistency, pipe a small circle on top of the centre and flood the outer of the circle flooding three-quarters of the ball. Allow to dry. Mix 1 part egg yellow food colouring with 6 parts spirits. Paint flooded area. Dip in castor sugar. Allow to dry.

PETAL

Make *1*

Cut 2 shapes with the larger daisy cutter and 3 shapes with the smaller daisy cutter. Store shapes in container. Take 1 small shape and, using scissors, snip a 'V' out of each of the 8 petals, making 16 petals. Place on foam. Press large pinhead into the centre to achieve a cup shape. Use eggwhite and a small brush to moisten the centre of the flower.

Insert a stem with the completed flower centre into the middle of the petal ring and pull it through so as the centre sits encircled by the petals. Secure petals to centre with your fingertips.

Take another small shape from the container and cut every second petal smaller. Place on foam. Press the centre of each petal with the small pinhead to

Golden Everlasting

achieve a cup-like effect. The smaller petals should curve more into the centre than the longer petals. Press the large pinhead into centre of flower to form a cup shape. Moisten the middle and insert flower on stem as you did before.

Repeat with the third smallest shape but do not cut petals and again place petals around the previous shape.

Take 1 large shape from the container and place on foam. Curve individual petals and cup flower as before. Insert flower on stem as before. Place petals in between previous petals. Repeat with the second large shape.

CLOSED BUD
Make *2*

Roll out modelling paste thinly. Using the small daisy cutter cut 1 shape. Roll it into a ball. Hook one end of the wire. Moisten hook with eggwhite and insert into ball. Mould ball into tear shape leaving the top pointed. Allow to dry.

Cut another shape with the small daisy cutter. Using scissors snip slightly in between each petal to lengthen. Place on foam. Press the small pinhead into every second petal to curve them up and towards the centre of the flower. With a small brush and the eggwhite, moisten the centre of the flower, the curved petals and the underside of the flat petals. Insert stem of bud through the middle of the flower.

Using your fingertips secure the flower at the base of the bud. Press curved petals into the bud and close.

OPEN BUD
Make *2*

Make a closed bud and then cut 2 small daisy shapes. With the first shape, cut every second petal smaller and slightly snip in between each petal. Place on foam. Press the small pinhead into smaller petals to curve petals up and towards centre. Moisten flower centre and insert stem. Secure the flower at the base of the bud with your fingertips.

With the second shape, slighty snip in between petals and place on foam. Curve petals inwards as above. Press large pinhead into centre to make a cup shape. Moisten centre with eggwhite and insert stem. Secure at base of bud. Allow to dry.

To colour flower and both buds, mix 1 part each of lemon yellow and egg yellow food colouring with 12 parts spirits. Paint all the petals on the flower and both types of buds with a medium paintbrush. Allow to dry. To colour the flower further, mix 1 part caramel brown food colouring with 2 parts water. Using a fine paintbrush smudge a line down the centre of each petal, back and front, on the two outer circles, then smudge the tips of all petals, large and small. With the same mixture, smudge a line on the centre back of the outer petals of both the closed and open buds.

Golden Everlasting

LEAF
Make 7

The leaves are different lengths (between 3 and 5 cm) and are twisted to different shapes. Roll a small amount of green modelling past into an oblong shape. Moisten end of fine wire with eggwhite. Insert moistened end of wire halfway through the oblong shape. Flatten oblong shape with rolling pin. Using the 3 smallest waterlily cutters, cut 2 large, 1 medium and 4 small leaves. Using a pin, etch a vein down the centre. Slightly twist each leaf to give individual shape. Allow to dry.

To colour the leaves, mix 1 part caramel brown and 1 part leaf green food colouring with 5 parts spirits. Paint the sides and tops of leaves. Allow to dry. Mix the chalks, 1 part sky blue with 2 parts grey and 1 part white, and dust the entire leaf.

ASSEMBLY

Take 1 open bud and position a closed bud on either side but just below the open bud. Secure with stem wrap about 1.5 cm below base of open bud. Position 1 medium and 2 large leaves behind cluster. Secure 1 flower and 1 open bud just below cluster of buds. Add 4 small leaves at different levels below the flower.

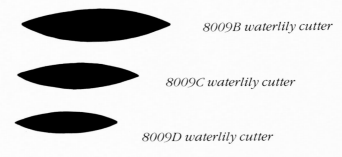

8009B waterlily cutter

8009C waterlily cutter

8009D waterlily cutter

Small 8 petal daisy cutter

Large 8 petal daisy cutter

HAPPY BIRTHDAY MARK

The ever popular koala and other Australian native animals enhance the flood work on this novelty birthday cake, which also features the flowering gum.

Flowering Gum

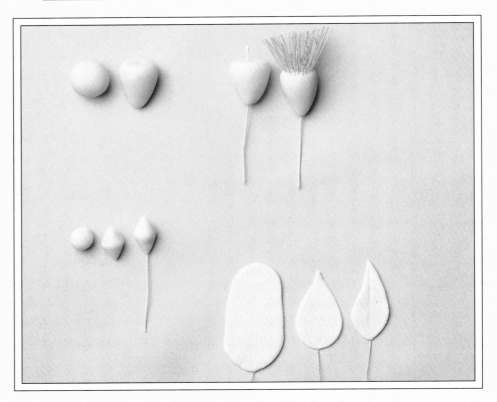

Materials

*large pinhead; green modelling paste; needle; thick
and medium wire; eggwhite; 1 thick tipped stamen
for each flower; coloured stamens (red or yellow) 7
cm long; medium paintbrush; leaf green, rose pink,
caramel brown and egg yellow liquid food
colouring; rolling pin; TO4 petal cutters; scissors;
skewer; spirits; dark orange chalk; brush for
dusting; green parafilm stem wrap*

FLOWER
Make *1*

Roll a ball the size of the large pinhead. Make a cone
shape about 1.5 cm high with the modelling paste.
Make a hole with a needle in the centre of the
pointed end of the cone. Dip hooked end of thick
wire in eggwhite and insert at least halfway into the
core. Press cone gently to secure wire.

Place a thick tipped stamen in the centre of the top
of the cone. Position coloured stamens (red or
yellow) in a circle around the centre stamen. Work
in circles towards the outer edge of the cone.
Position stamens in between stamens of previous
circles rather than in rows. Allow to dry.

BUD
Make *3*

Make a ball of paste about the size of a large pea.
Mould into a diamond shape by positioning two
fingers on top and two fingers on the bottom and
rotating ball to a point at either end. Make a hole
with a pin on one end. Moisten hooked end of thick
wire with eggwhite and insert in hole about halfway
through. Allow to dry.

To colour both flower and bud, paint the top and a
third of the side with undiluted leaf green
colouring. Rinse brush in water. Paint the bottom
third with rose pink undiluted food colouring.
Rinse brush. Paint the middle with undiluted egg
yellow food colouring. With the clean damp brush,
paint the cone unevenly to combine colours. Paint
the middle stamen leaf green.

Flowering Gum

LEAF
Make 3

Roll a small amount of paste into an oblong shape. Moisten end of medium wire with eggwhite. Insert wire halfway through. Flatten leaf with rolling pin. Cut with TO4 B cutter and then trim it with scissors to resemble a gumleaf. Vein centre of leaf with needle. Dry leaf lengthwise over skewer so it dries in a more realistic shape.

To colour, mix 2 parts leaf green and 1 part caramel brown liquid food colouring with 8 parts spirits, to achieve a dark green colour. Paint entire leaf and allow to dry. Dust edge and centre vein with dark orange chalk.

ASSEMBLY

Secure 2 leaves together, allowing 1 leaf to sit slightly higher. Position flowering gum and 1 bud just below the base of the leaves. Secure with stem wrap. Add 2 buds just below the flowering gum and a leaf either side of the buds. Secure with stem wrap.

TO4 B cutter

Rosemary Grevillea

Materials

size 1 piping tube and bag; waxed paper; royal icing; fine wire; small scissors; fine paintbrush; rose pink, pillar box red, caramel brown and leaf green liquid food colouring; spirits; modelling paste; rolling pin; small pinhead; green parafilm stem wrap

CLOSED FLOWER
Make 3

With icing at soft peak consistency, pipe 3 pairs of grevillea on to waxed paper. Start to pipe from centre curl and build up at the base to give the effect of a bulb.

When dry, join pairs together with firm consistency royal icing either side of a 4 cm length of hooked wire.

OPEN FLOWER
Make 4

Cut 4 5 cm lengths of wire. Dip the tops of wire into very soft royal icing to form a small dot. Allow to dry. Pipe 4 pairs of grevillea.

When dry, place pairs together with firm consis-

tency royal icing, the wire protruding 2 cm above the flower. Pinch halves at centre back, slightly separating pairs to open flower. Fill bottom opening with royal icing to form a bulb. Tidy up and round off bulb with a paintbrush.

To colour flowers, paint bottom halves with a mixture of 1 part rose pink and 1 part pillar box red food colouring with 10 parts spirits.

Colour the top halves with 1 part rose pink and 1 part pillar box red food colouring with 20 parts spirits. They can, in fact, be painted various colours, including yellow.

LEAF
Make 7

Roll balls of modelling paste half the size of the small pinhead over the top of 7 4 cm lengths of wire to

Rosemary Grevillea

form narrow, cylindrical pointed leaves 1.5 cm long. Allow to dry.

To colour, paint with a mixture of 1 part caramel brown and 2 parts leaf green food colouring with 10 parts spirits.

  flower

ASSEMBLY

Twist 4 leaves together, then twist the open flowers together and place in front of leaves. Next, twist the closed flowers together and place these in front of the open flowers. Finally, twist 3 leaves together, place them in front of the closed flowers and secure the spray with stem wrap.

Cooktown Orchid

Materials

*49C orchid throat cutter; airtight container;
medium wire; eggwhite; tweezers; yellow, pink,
royal blue and maroon chalk; brush for dusting;
scissors; foam; medium and large pinhead; satay
stick; 8609 large calyx cutter; silver snowflake
glitter; 74a mini orchid cutter; tin foil*

*49C orchid
throat cutter*

8609 large calyx cutter

TONGUE PETAL
Make *1*

Cut two shapes with the orchid throat cutter. Store
one shape in container and roll the other into a ball.
Hook wire on one end. Moisten hook of wire with
eggwhite and insert wire halfway into ball. Mould
ball into cylinder. Lightly flatten with fingertips.
Using tweezers, pinch the top to achieve a cobra
head shape. Slightly bend shape forward. It should
be approximately 1.5cm long.

To colour, dust with yellow chalk.

THROAT PETAL
Make *1*

Take the second shape from the container. Using
scissors, slightly snip side of arms. Place on foam.
Using the medium pinhead, press into the tip of one

arm and bring pinhead down to base of shape.
Repeat with other arm. This curves both arms up.
Place satay stick on centre of shape and roll once to
the left and once to the right, to slightly flatten.
Moisten the base of the throat petal with eggwhite
and place base of tongue petal on moistened area.
Secure by pinching base with fingertips and close
the arms of the throat petal around the tongue petal.
Allow to dry.

To colour, dust sides and top with 5 parts pink and 1
part maroon chalk with 2 parts snowflake glitter.

LARGE BUD
Make *2*

Make a ball the size of the large pinhead and shape it
into a long teardrop. Moisten hooked end of wire
and insert halfway through teardrop. Secure base
with fingertips by gently pressing. Using the

Cooktown Orchid

Floral emblem of Queensland

74 a mini orchid cutter

scissors, snip each side of the bud to create a petal effect.

Roll out a small amount of modelling paste thinly. Cut out shape with large calyx cutter. Cut bottom two petals off the shape and discard. Place the shape on foam. Press each petal with the medium pinhead to create a cup shape. Moisten the base of each petal and wrap shape around prepared bud. Leave petals slightly open.

SMALL BUD
Make *2*

Roll a ball half the size of the ball used for the large bud. Moisten hooked end of wire and insert halfway through the ball. Shape ball as shown. Allow to dry.

To colour buds, dust all over with chalk and glitter mixture.

FLOWER
Make *1*

Cut one shape with the orchid cutter. Slightly snip a thin 'V' where side petals meet the top petal. Using your fingertips, slightly pinch closed the top

pointed petal and the two bottom pointed petals closed to create a vein on each. Flute the two side petals slightly and vein, using a satay stick.

Make a hollow in the centre of a circle of tin foil. Place orchid shape on top of foil. Using your fingertips, slightly push the two side petals towards the centre and slightly bend backwards. Press the medium pinhead in centre of flower. Lightly moisten centre of flower with eggwhite. Insert throat petal into centre of flower, pushing wire through. Pinch base of flower to secure. Allow to dry in tin foil.

To colour, dust flower with the same chalk and glitter mix used on the buds.

ASSEMBLY

Start at the top with the buds, alternating small with large and then add the flower.

Alpine Bluebell

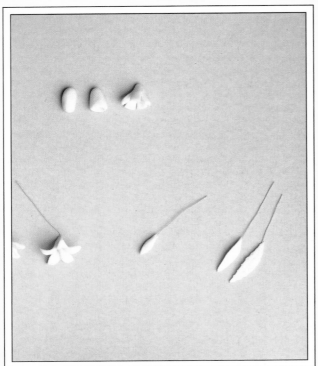

Floral emblem of Australian Capital Territory

Materials

*modelling paste; small and medium pinheads; fine
wire; white, mauve and blue chalk; brush for chalk;
small rolling pin; scissors; skewer; royal icing; leaf
green and caramel brown liquid food colouring;
scalpel; medium paintbrush; spirits*

FLOWER
Make 3

Make centre stamen first by rolling a ball of paste
half the size of the small pinhead to a fine point 1.5
cm long, over a piece of wire. Allow to dry. Dust
with white chalk.

Roll paste the size of the medium pinhead into shape
shown and hollow to form a cone. Cut the open end
5 times to form petals, cutting two thirds of the way
down.

Shape petals to a point, flatten and vein lengthwise
with skewer. Press the small pinhead into the flower
centre to give a hollowed effect. Insert wired stamen
into flower, curl petals back and firm at base.

Colour flowers with equal parts of blue and mauve
chalk.

BUD
Make 3

Mould a small pinhead of paste into bud shape over a

piece of hooked wire and vein with a scalpel.

Dust top with blue and mauve chalk mixture. Then
paint a 5 pointed calyx on the base of flower and
bud with soft consistency pale green royal icing.

LEAF
Make 3

Place a small pinhead of paste over wire. Roll to
about 2 cm long and cut to shape. Make small cuts
on edges of leaves, vein and bend slightly to dry.

Paint leaves with 2 parts leaf green and 1 part
caramel brown liquid food colouring with 10 parts
spirits.

ASSEMBLY

Simply twist 3 flowers, 3 buds and 3 leaves together.

'HAPPY BIRTHDAY ADAM' GUMNUT BABY CAKE
First prize Whittlesea Show 1988.
Just watch your children's faces light up when they see this striking gumnut baby gathering set
off with bright Sturt's Desert Pea, flowering gum, Dagger Wattle and gumnuts.

33

Eucalyptus Blue Gum

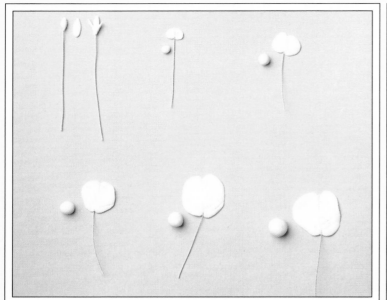

Materials

*fine and thick wire; small pinhead; modelling
paste; small rolling pin; scissors; leaf green and
caramel liquid food colouring; medium
paintbrush; spirits; leaf green, blue and red chalk;
cornflour; brush for dusting*

LEAF BUD
Make *2*

Put a small hook in the top of a piece of thick wire
10 cm long. Place a half small pinhead of paste over
the hook and shape into an oval bud. Cut 2 tiny oval
leaves and place either side of the bud.

LEAF
Make *18*

Place a half small pinhead of paste over fine wire,
then flatten, roll out, shape as shown and vein to
form leaf. Make 4 leaves this size. Then make 5 to 7
pairs of leaves for each stem, increasing the size each
time.

Paint all leaves with a mixture of 2 parts leaf green
and 1 part caramel brown food colouring with 40
parts spirits.

When dry, dust with 1 part each of leaf green and
blue chalk and 2 parts cornflour. Dust edges with
red chalk.

ASSEMBLY

Place leaf bud at the top of each stem, then place
pairs of leaves around wire, alternately facing side to
side, front to back, starting with the smallest set at
the top. Secure stems together as shown.

CONGRATULATIONS DAVID

An FJ Holden, sprays of Fuchsia Gum, Eucalyptus Blue Gum and wattle adorn this 21st cake.
Fuchsia Gum decorates a delicate bird plaque. A painting and a spray of wattle and Eucalyptus for the budding artist.

Waratah

Materials

*modelling paste; pillar box red, rose pink, leaf
green and caramel brown liquid food colouring;
spirits; paintbrush; fine, medium and thick wire;
scissors; small, medium and large pinheads; 35b
heart cutter; rolling pin; 8009 small and medium
waterlily cutters; corn husk; foil; green parafilm
stem wrap; leaf green chalk; brush for dusting*

FLOWER
Make 1

Colour paste with pillar box red food colouring.
Put a small hook in the top of a 9 cm length of thick
wire. Mould a ball of paste the size of the small
pinhead into an oval shape as shown over the wire.
Make 5 more about 7 mm long, and place around
and slightly lower than centre shape. Place a second
row of 10 shapes, about 1 cm long around centre,
again making the tops slightly lower than the
previous row.

Roll another 10 shapes, with balls the size of the
medium pinhead, rolling between fingers to form a
small bulb at the top. These should be about 1.5 cm
long. Place around centre, slightly lower than the
previous row.

Roll 10 more balls the same size on the fine hooked
wire, rolling between fingers to form a small bulb at
the top of a 1.8 cm long shape. Place on to flower as
before but turn in slightly towards the centre. Allow
to dry.

To colour, paint with 1 part each of pillar box red
and rose pink food colouring with 6 parts spirits.

Roll 16 narrow pieces of paste from balls the size of
the small pinhead, on to fine hooked wire 5 cm
long. Form a bulb at the top and bend slightly to dry.
Cut 16 small heart shapes and flute with fingers
around top edge to make petals finer. Moisten base
of petal and wrap around wired shape. Allow to dry.

To colour, paint with same red and pink mixture as
above. Place around flower slightly lower than
previous row.

Waratah

Floral emblem of New South Wales

PETAL
Make *14*

Place a ball of paste the size of the medium pinhead over a piece of fine wire. Roll and cut 7 petals with the small waterlily cutter, vein with corn husk and dry with a slight bend over a piece of foil. Repeat, making another 7 petals with the medium waterlily cutter. Allow to dry.

To colour, paint with the same mixture as before. Place the small petals around the flower, then the larger petals. Cover wires with stem wrap. Brush top of flower with a touch of leaf green chalk.

LEAF
Make *5*

Leaves are long and serrated. Place a ball of paste the size of the large pinhead over medium wire 5 cm long. Roll, cut to shape shown, vein and bend slightly to dry.

To colour, paint with 2 parts leaf green and 1 part caramel brown liquid food colouring with 8 parts spirits.

ASSEMBLY

Simply place 5 leaves on stem with flower. Secure with stem wrap.

8009B waterlily cutter

8009C waterlily cutter

35b heart cutter

Donkey Orchid

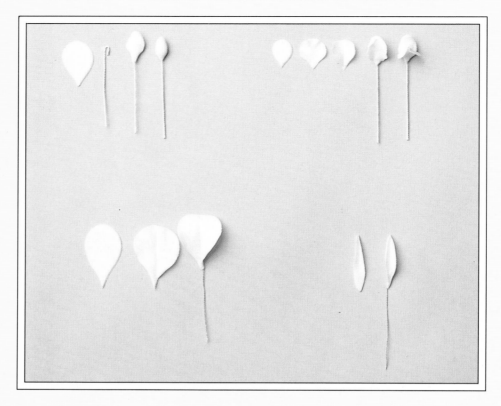

Materials

white modelling paste; small rolling pin; T04 petal cutters; fine and medium wire; eggwhite; satay stick; foam; cream, maroon, green and yellow chalk; 8009D waterlily cutter ; T12 E cutter; leaf green and lemon yellow liquid food colouring; spirits; fine and medium paintbrushes; airtight container; scissors; white parafilm stem wrap

TONGUE PETAL
Make 3

Roll out the paste. Using the T04 D petal cutter, cut out 1 shape. Roll it into a ball. Moisten the hooked end of the medium wire with eggwhite, and insert wire halfway into ball. Make a teardrop shape. Using your fingertips, lightly flatten the teardrop. Pinch the outer edges and slightly bend the top inwards.

THROAT PETAL
Make 3

Using the T04 E petal cutter, cut 1 shape. Slightly flute out edges with satay stick. Fold petal in half lengthwise. The impression made with the satay stick should be on the outside. Moisten the base of the throat with eggwhite, and place petal on the base of tongue petal. Secure by holding the base between your fingertips, then gently bring the top half of the throat down. Allow to dry thoroughly.

EAR PETAL
Make 6

Using the T04 C petal cutter, cut 1 shape. Using a satay stick, lightly flute around the edges. Fold petal in half to create the centre vein. Moisten the tip of the fine wire and, holding the base of the petal between your fingertips, insert it. Secure wire by pressing base of petal. Slightly bend top of petal outwards. Allow to dry with the top of the petal hanging over the edge of the foam.

To colour, dust back and front with cream chalk. Using the fine brush and the maroon chalk lightly colour the vein down the centre and around the very edge. Colour the base with the medium brush.

Donkey Orchid

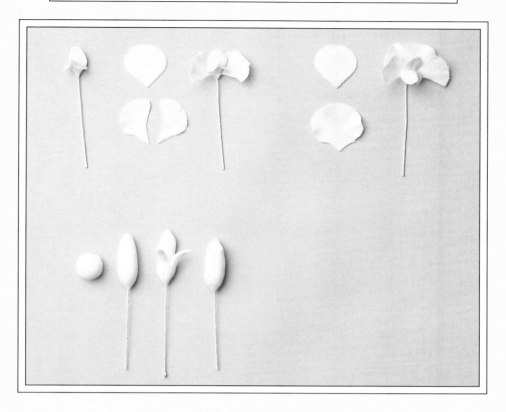

LONG PETAL
Make 6

Using the waterlily cutter, cut 1 shape. Gently roll satay stick along the shape. Pinch the pointed end. Holding the top of the shape between your fingertips, insert moistened tip of fine wire quarter of the way into the pointed end. Secure wire by partly folding petal in half. Allow to dry.

To colour, dust the top half of the petal with maroon and the bottom half with green chalk.

FLOWER
Make 3

Start with the combined throat and tongue petal. Cut 2 shapes with the T12 E cutter. Cut one shape in half lengthwise and place the second shape in container. Slightly flute the outside and the top half of the inside edge of both halves with a satay stick. Moisten the tip of the base of each half with eggwhite. Secure one half, with the rounded edge on top, to the back and side of the combined throat and tongue petal. Secure the other half in the same way on the other side, overlapping the first half.

Take second shape from container and slightly flute the outer edges. Put eggwhite on the tip of its base.

Secure the base of the petal to the base of the flower. Hold the base of the flower between your fingertips and gently press the top of the petal back as shown. Allow to dry.

To colour, dust the tongue and centre of the flower with yellow chalk. Using the medium brush and the maroon chalk, lightly dust around the edges of the petals. Dust the throat heavily with maroon. Dust the back of the flower with cream chalk.

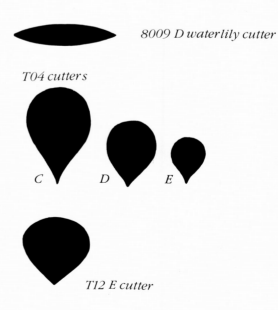

8009 D waterlily cutter

T04 cutters

C   D   E

T12 E cutter

Donkey Orchid

BUD
Make 3

Roll a paste ball the size of a large pea, then into a sausage shape with a slight point on top. Moisten the hooked end of medium wire with eggwhite. Insert moistened end of wire halfway in and pinch the base to secure wire. Using the scissors, snip halfway down the length on one side of the shape, taking a third of the side out from it. Snip this third down the middle, making 2 pieces extending from the shape. Roll the satay stick on the inside of each to flatten. Gently pinch the outside of each to make a groove on the inside. Using the scissors again, vein the tip of the shape with 4 lines down the sides. Bring the 2 extensions back up, but leave separate. Slightly bend the 2 tips outwards. This gives the impression of the bud opening.

To colour, paint the entire bud with 1 part lemon yellow and 1 part leaf green liquid food colouring mixed with 25 parts spirits. Allow to dry.

ASSEMBLY

Place the ear petals behind the flower, so they protrude three-quarters above the top of the flower. Secure with stem wrap. Place the long petals at the base of the flower. Secure with stem wrap and gently adjust petals to point downwards. Assemble 3 flowers and arrange with buds as you like in a spray.

CAROL

This pale pink oval cake features a spray of Native Fuchsia, Tea Tree, Geraldton Wax and Pink Ice Protea.

Philotheca

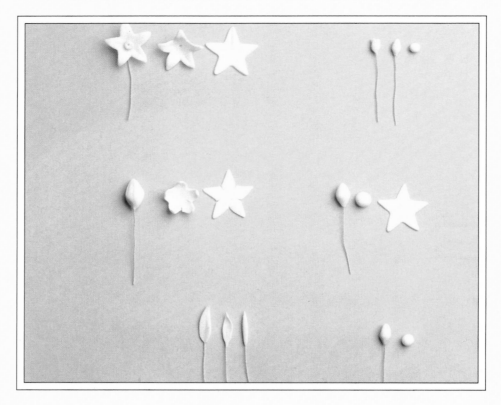

Materials

*modelling paste; small and medium pinheads; fine
wire; eggwhite; small pin; scissors; 7082 hyacinth
cutter; foam; airtight container; leaf green liquid
food colouring; medium paintbrush; small rolling
pin; yellow, light green, mauve and pink chalk;
cornflour; brush for dusting; green parafilm
stem wrap*

FLOWER
Make 3

To make the flower centre, roll a small ball of
modelling paste slightly smaller than the small
pinhead. Hook one end of wire. Moisten hooked
end with eggwhite and insert end halfway through
the ball. Secure the wire by gently pressing the base
of ball. Mould ball into a teardrop shape, point at the
top. With a pin make an indentation in centre top of
teardrop shape. Snip around the identation with fine
scissors to give the effect of delicate stamens. Allow
to dry.

Roll out more paste thinly. Cut three flowers with
hyacinth cutter. Using a pin, mark each petal with a
centre vein. Lay flowers on foam. Press the centre of
the flower into the foam with the medium pinhead
to bring the petals up, at the same time using your
fingertips gently to press tips of petals back down
towards foam. Using the smallest amount of eggwhite you can, slightly moisten the centre of the
flower. Thread stem and centre piece through the
centre of the flower. Gently press base of flower to
secure centre piece. Allow to dry.

LARGE BUD
Make 1

Cut a shape with the cutter and roll it into a ball.
Attach bud to wire and shape to a point at either
end. Allow to dry. Roll out a small amount of
modelling paste. Cut out shape with cutter. Snip in
between petals then press into foam to curve petals
upward. Moisten inside with eggwhite. Insert stem
with bud through the centre of petals and push to
base of bud. Fold petal numbers 2 and 5 over the
bud. Press remaining petals close to the bud, but
leave slightly opened.

SMALL BUD
Make 2

Roll a small ball of modelling paste the size of the
medium pinhead and half the size of a large bud. Dip
hooked end of wire in eggwhite and insert it
halfway through the ball. Shape ball into a teardrop
shape, and secure stem to bud. Mark the top of the
bud with fine scissors to give the effect of petals.
Allow to dry.

Philotheca

LEAF
Make *4* small
Make *10* large

Colour modelling paste leaf green. Make a small ball of paste and roll into long shape. Moisten one end of wire with eggwhite and insert halfway into paste. Roll paste between two fingers and the palm of your hand. Nip off the top and bottom and roll again (this thins out the paste). Repeat until you have a leaf about 1 cm long or, for a large leaf, 2 cm long. Lightly flatten with a rolling pin.

To colour flower and buds, mix 1 part yellow with 2 parts light green chalk. Dust the base of buds and flowers. Next, mix 1 part mauve and 2 parts pink chalk with 1 part cornflour. Lightly dust the inside of the base of the petals. Dust tips of petals heavier, so the colour is slightly darker. Mix 1 part yellow with 2 parts light green chalk. Dust the centre of each flower. Then dust the rest of the flowers and buds.

ASSEMBLY

Attach 2 small leaves slightly below the base of a small bud. Attach 2 longer leaves slightly lower and in between the small leaves. Attach 1 large bud and 1 long leaf about 1 cm down the stem. Attach a flower 1 cm further down the stem. Add another flower and 2 long leaves, 5 mm further down the stem, placing the leaves either side of flower. For the second spray, start off as before with a small bud and 2 small leaves. Then lower down the stem attach the longer leaves with 1 flower between them. Attach the 2 sprays together, with the flowers level. Stem wrap remainder of stem.

7082 hyacinth cutter

Tasmanian Blue Gum

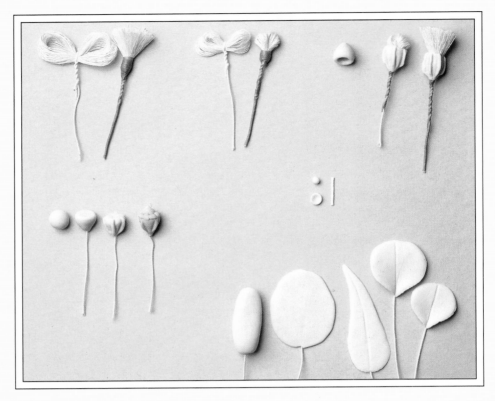

Materials

*medium wire; cream coloured cotton; green
parafilm stem wrap; small and medium pinheads;
small amount of grey and green modelling paste;
modelling tool or skewer; foam; small rolling pin;
eggwhite; tweezers; size 1 tube and piping bag;
royal icing; thick stamens; light grey, light blue,
khaki, dark orange, lime green and dark brown
chalk; cornflour; brush for dusting; T12 E and D
cutters; small pin; scissors; T04 A cutter*

FLOWER
Make 2

Follow the directions for making the flower of the
Red Flowering Gum on page 52, but once you have
secured the stem in the cone, pinch the sides with
tweezers to form 6 ridges.

OPEN BUD
Make 1

Again, follow the directions for making the open
bud of the Red Flowering Gum on page 52, but fold
the cotton loops up, not down along the stem. Make
the cone in the same way as for the flower.

CLOSED BUD
Make 1

Roll a ball of grey modelling paste slightly larger
than the medium pinhead. Hook one end of a length

of wire, moisten it with eggwhite and insert halfway
into the paste. Shape ball into a cone, flat on top.
Hold it upside down and pinch sides with tweezers
to make 6 ridges. Allow to dry.

Pipe a circle of small blobs around the edge of the
top of the cone with grey royal icing mixed to a firm
peak consistency. Pipe a large blob in the centre.
Allow to dry.

To colour flower and buds, mix equal parts of light
grey, light blue chalk and cornflour. Dust flowers
and buds completely.

STAMEN
Make 2

Using the green modelling paste, roll a ball half the
size of the small pinhead. Place on foam. Flatten ball
with small pinhead and moisten the base with
eggwhite. Place flattened shape in the centre of the
flower and press lightly with the small pinhead to

Tasmanian Blue Gum

Floral emblem of Tasmania

secure it. The cotton should now be spread evenly. Moisten one end of a 1 cm length of stamen, with the tip cut off, with eggwhite. Insert moistened end into the centre of the flower, i.e. through the modelling paste.

LEAF

Make *2* mature
Make *4* young

For the mature leaves, roll a small amount of green modelling paste into a sausage shape. Moisten one end of medium wire with eggwhite and insert three-quarters of the way through. Flatten sausage with rolling pin. Ensure wire is placed in the centre of the flattened leaf. Cut flattened shape with T04 A cutter. Trim with scissors and shape by slightly curving. Etch a vein down centre of leaf with a pin. Allow to dry. Use the same method for the young leaves, using grey modelling paste, but cut 4 flattened leaves with T12 E and D cutters — 2 of each. The peak should be at the base. Pinch the base of the leaf to create a more rounded effect. Etch a vein down the centre of the leaf using a pin. Allow to dry by hanging top of leaf over edge of foam.

To colour mature leaves, mix equal parts of lime green, khaki and dark brown chalk. Dust entire leaf. Dust edges and centre vein with dark orange chalk.

To colour young leaves, mix equal parts of light grey, light blue, khaki chalk and cornflour. Dust entire leaf. Use dark orange chalk to dust edges and centre vein.

ASSEMBLY

Tape both mature leaves together allowing 1 leaf to sit slightly higher. Position 1 flower and open bud at the base of the higher leaf and tape with stem wrap. Place closed bud and a small young leaf just below the flower and open bud and secure. Position another flower and large young leaf just below and secure. Place remaining leaves just below and secure with stem wrap.

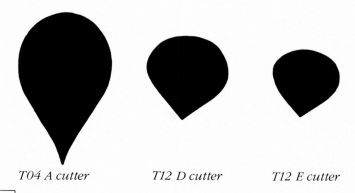

T04 A cutter   T12 D cutter   T12 E cutter

Correa

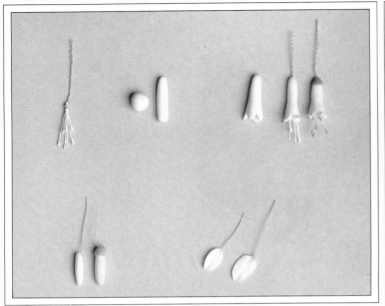

Materials

fine wire; fine stamens; scissors; small and medium pinheads; modelling paste; small rolling pin; skewer; lime green chalk; cornflour; brush for dusting; caramel brown and leaf green liquid food colouring; fine paintbrush; royal icing; spirits; green parafilm stem wrap

FLOWER
Make *3*

Using fine wire 7 cm long, tie together 4 stamens and 1 topless stamen 2.5 cm long and 4 stamens cut to 1.5 cm long.

Mould a ball of paste the size of the medium pinhead into a cylindrical shape 2 cm long. Insert skewer and hollow to form a long bell.

Cut open end into 4 petals 5 mm long. Shape petals by pointing ends, then flatten and vein with skewer. Thread wired stamens through flower, then pinch firm at base. Turn petals outwards to curve slightly.

BUD
Make *3*

Mould different sized cylindrical shapes between 1-1.5 cm long on to hooked wire.

When dry, dust flowers and buds with 1 part very pale lime green chalk and 2 parts cornflour, inside and out, and paint the stamen tips pale caramel brown. Paint a small calyx with soft caramel brown royal icing at base of flowers and buds.

LEAF
Make *12*

Roll a small pinhead of paste over a piece of wire. Using scissors, cut to shape shown, and vein. Mould leaves in different sizes, 1-2 cm long.

To colour, paint with 2 parts leaf green and 1 part caramel brown food colouring with 8 parts spirits.

ASSEMBLY

Twist 3 small leaves and 1 small bud together at the top of the stem and then work down the stem adding leaves and buds increasing in size. Then add flowers, finishing off with 2 or 3 leaves. Secure with stem wrap.

HAPPY BIRTHDAY TONY

This arrangement of Australian natives would be suitable for a birthday, welcome home or bon voyage cake.
Highlighting this spray are Scarlet Banksia, Barrier Range Wattle, flowering gum and gumnuts.

Red Bottlebrush

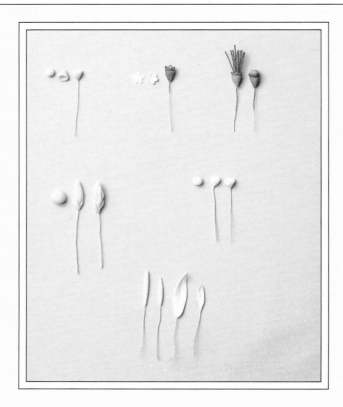

Materials

*modelling paste; small and medium pinheads;
modelling tool or skewer; 5 cm lengths fine wire
and 7 cm lengths medium wire; eggwhite; small
rolling pin; 7093 forget-me-not cutter; airtight
container; foam; small pin; leaf green, caramel
brown, pillar box red, rose pink and egg yellow
liquid food colouring; spirits; fine paintbrush;
stamens; paper towel; size 1 piping tube and bag;
royal icing; scissors; light green, light brown
and red chalk; brush for dusting; green parafilm
stem wrap*

FLOWER
Make 24

With modelling paste make a ball slightly larger than
the small pinhead. Shape ball into a cone. Hollow
with modelling tool or skewer. Hook one end of fine
wire, moisten it with eggwhite and insert it through
the centre of cone. Secure hooked end at the base of
the cone. Allow to dry. You will need 30 of these, 1
for each flower and 6 more for each bud.

Roll out paste thinly. Using the forget-me-not cutter,
cut 30 shapes. Store shapes in container. Taking one
shape at a time, place on foam and press each petal
and centre with the small pinhead to create a cup-
like effect. Lightly moisten inside and top edge of
prepared cone shape with eggwhite. Place cup
shape on moistened area of the cone and gently
press it into the cone using the small pinhead. Pierce

the centre of the cup shape with a small pin and
rotate to open.

To colour, mix 2 parts leaf green and 1 part caramel
brown liquid food colouring with 15 parts spirits.
Paint the prepared cones. Allow to dry.

Snip the tops off stamens. Cut 288 stamens to 1.25
cm, leaving 24 stamens long. Place all stamens in a
mixture of 1 part pillar box red and 1 part rose pink
food colouring with 4 parts spirits. Place on a paper
towel to dry. Fill the centre of 24 cones with green
royal icing mixed to medium peak consistency.
Insert about 12 stamens in each with a long stamen
in the centre. Allow to dry. Trim stamens to 1 cm in
length, but leaving the centre stamen about 5 mm
longer than the others.

Red Bottlebrush

BUD
Make *6*

Fill the centre of each cone with red royal icing mixed to medium peak consistency. The icing should protrude out of the centre. Allow to dry.

To colour, mix 1 part pillar box red with 1 part rose pink liquid food colouring. Paint the icing centre.

LEAF CLUSTER
Make *1*

Roll a ball of modelling paste slightly larger than the medium pinhead. Moisten hooked end of medium wire and insert halfway through the ball. Shape ball into a teardrop about 1.5 cm long. Starting at the base of the teardrop pinch around the sides with scissor points 3 times. Repeat this process working up the sides of the teardrop, pinching in between previous levels to make 5 levels in all. Allow to dry.

To colour, dust cluster with light green chalk. Then dust each individual leaf tip on bottom 3 levels with light brown chalk. The remaining individual leaf tips should be dusted with red chalk.

 7903 forget-me-not cutter

LEAF
Make *6* small
Make *16* large

Make a small ball of paste and roll into a long thin cylinder. Moisten one end of a length of fine wire with eggwhite and insert halfway into paste. Roll paste between two fingers and the palm of your hand. Nip off the top and bottom and roll again to thin out. Repeat until you have a leaf about 1 cm in length. Lightly flatten with a rolling pin. Make 6 this size and a further 16 leaves 2 cm long.

To colour leaves light green, mix 2 parts leaf green and 1 part caramel brown food colouring with about 12 parts spirits, then paint. Allow to dry.

ASSEMBLY

Place 3 small leaves just below the leaf cluster and secure with stem wrap. Place 3 large leaves just below, to overlap half of the smaller leaves. Next, place 3 buds in a circle just below the leaves. Add another 3 buds just under and in between the first level of buds. Place 3 flowers below and in between buds, remembering to secure all leaves with stem wrap. Repeat with remaining flowers, moving down the stem at all times. Attach 2 large leaves just below the level of flowers. Continue down the stem for a further 4 levels, positioning leaves around the stem. When bottlebrush is assembled, tip flower stamens with flooding consistency white royal icing using a fine paintbrush. When dry, paint red bottlebrush tips with a mixture of 1 part egg yellow food colouring and 20 parts spirits.

Christmas Bell

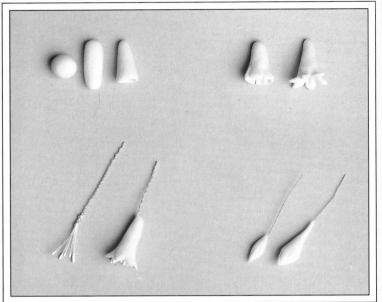

Materials

*modelling paste; large pinhead; rolling pin;
skewer or modelling tool; scissors; fine stamens;
egg yellow, pillar box red and orange liquid food
colouring; spirits; paintbrush; fine wire; scalpel;
leaf green chalk; brush for dusting*

FLOWER
Make 3

With a ball of paste the size of the large pinhead, roll to shape shown — 2 cm long. With a skewer or modelling tool, hollow to a cone shape.

Make 6 small cuts about 5 mm deep to form 6 petals. Trim with scissors, then flatten with fingers, to thin out petals. Vein centre of each petal with modelling tool or skewer. Turn petals back slightly.

Wire 6 2 cm long stamens together. Place rounded end of skewer or modelling tool into cone to give a good shape. Pull stamens through flower. Secure at base. Allow to dry.

To colour, paint inside and half outside of flower with a mixture of 1 part egg yellow food colouring and 20 parts spirits. Then paint outside of bell with a mixture of 1 part pillar box red colouring and 4 parts spirits, blending into the yellow. Paint stamens with a mixture of 1 part each of orange and egg yellow food colouring and 6 parts spirits.

BUD
Make 3

Mould bud shape over hooked wire, making 6 cuts in the top with scalpel. Make buds varying in size from the medium to large pinhead.

Paint the same as the flower, brushing a little pale leaf green chalk on the top.

ASSEMBLY

Simply twist 3 buds together, then 3 flowers further down the stem.

WEDDING CAKE
First prize Whittlesea Show 1988.
Donkey Orchids, Pink Boronia and white Happy Wanderer make an elegant spray and eye-catching colouring combination on this beautiful cake. Piping is kept to a minimum to emphasise the flowers.

Red Flowering Gum

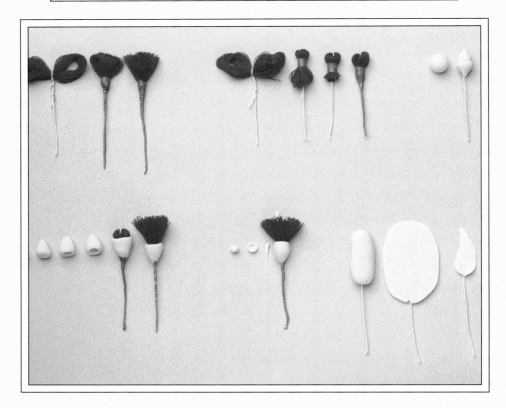

Materials

*7 cm medium wire lengths; cream, orange or red
cotton; green parafilm stem wrap; small, medium
and large pinheads; modelling paste; modelling
tool or skewer; foam; small rolling pin; eggwhite;
leaf green, caramel brown, rose pink and egg
yellow liquid food colouring; medium paintbrush;
thick stamens; thick wire; scalpel; scissors; spirits*

FLOWER
Make *1*

Hook medium wire. Wrap cotton around 2 fingers
60 times. Remove cotton from fingers and halve
circle of cotton with hooked wire; twist to secure.
Wrap stem wrap just above the wire, twist and
continue wrapping down the stem. Cut tops off
cotton loops.

Make a ball slightly larger than the medium pinhead
with the modelling paste. Mould ball to a cone
shape. Using modelling tool or skewer, hollow
centre of cone. Insert small pinhead into hollow,
place cone on foam and roll to get a cup shape.
Moisten centre of cone with eggwhite and insert
stem through the centre so that the cotton protrudes
from the top. Lightly press base to secure. Allow to
dry.

Colour modelling paste lime green using egg yellow
and leaf green food colouring. Make a very small
ball half the size of the small pinhead. Flatten and
press in the centre with the small-sized pinhead to
make a small cup. Turn upside down and moisten it
with eggwhite. Press moistened side into the centre
of the flower. Moisten the end of one thick stamen
and insert into the centre.

OPEN BUD
Make *1*

Wrap cotton around 2 fingers 60 times. Remove
cotton from fingers and halve as before. Fold cotton
halves back on stem. Wrap a thin strip of stem wrap
halfway down length of cotton and secure firmly.
Trim the cotton which is below the stem wrap. Wrap
stem wrap from base of cotton to end of stem.

Make and fit cone on to the bud the same way you
did for the flower.

CLOSED BUD
Make *1*

Using modelling paste make a ball about half the size
of the large pinhead. Make a hole with a pin on one
end of the ball. Moisten hooked end of thick wire

Red Flowering Gum

with eggwhite and insert in hole about halfway through the ball. As you are securing the ball, mould into shape by positioning two fingers on top and two fingers on the bottom and rotating ball to a point at either end. Vein with scalpel around the top. Allow to dry.

To colour both flower and bud, follow directions on page 26 for colouring Flowering Gum. Both the open and closed buds may be made in white modelling paste and coloured green, or the paste may be coloured green first.

LEAF
Make 3

Roll a small amount of green modelling paste, slightly larger than the large pinhead, into a fat cylindrical shape. Moisten one end of medium wire with eggwhite. Insert end of wire halfway through. Flatten shape with rolling pin. Cut long and slender leaves with scissors, making a 2 cm, a 3 cm and a 4 cm long leaf. Vein centre of leaves with a pin. Dry them lengthwise over a skewer.

To colour the leaves, mix together 2 parts leaf green and 1 part caramel brown liquid food colouring with 8 parts spirits, to make a dark green colour. Paint entire leaf. Allow to dry.

ASSEMBLY

Take the small and medium leaves, placing the latter slightly lower and wrap together. Place flower in centre and open bud and large leaf on either side and wrap together. Then place closed bud in front below flower, and wrap remainder of stem.

Pink Ice Protea

Materials

modelling paste; medium pinhead; small rolling pin; 8009 A B and C waterlily cutters; leaf green and caramel brown liquid food colouring; spirits; paintbrush; dark pink, cream, purple, black, pink, brown and apricot chalk; brush for dusting; cornflour; toothpick; royal icing; size 00 piping tube and bag; T04 D petal cutter; foam; silver lustre; green parafilm stem wrap

LEAF

Make *8*

Place a ball of paste the size of the medium pinhead over fine wire. Roll, flatten and cut with largest waterlily cutter. Vein and curve to dry.

To colour, paint with 3 parts leaf green and 1 part caramel brown liquid food colouring with 12 parts spirits. When dry, dust with a little dark pink chalk on the top edges.

FLOWER

Make *1*

Mould and shape a large ball of modelling paste about 5 cm long and 3 cm wide at the base on to a toothpick. Allow to dry.

Using soft royal icing and piping tube, pipe lines over top half of centre starting halfway down and working up. Allow to dry.

Dust all over piping with cream chalk. Then dust with equal parts of dark pink chalk and cornflour on top half of piped lines. Dust directly on top of lines with a mixture of 2 parts dark pink, 2 parts purple and 1 part black chalk.

PETAL

Make *50*

Roll out modelling paste and cut 9 waterlily petals with the largest cutter.

Dust both sides with a mixture of 3 parts pink and 1 part brown chalk with 3 parts cornflour.

Pink Ice Protea

Place petal on foam and push a pinhead in the top of the petal to curve slightly. Moisten lower half of petal with eggwhite or water and place petals evenly around the flower centre. Allow to dry. This is best done upside down.

Cut 9 medium-sized waterlily petals. Colour the same as the large petals. Push a pinhead down the centre of each petal to cup slightly. Moisten and place below and alternating with the first row.

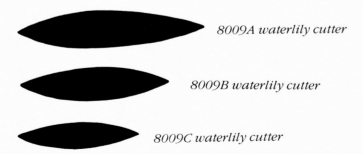

8009A waterlily cutter

8009B waterlily cutter

8009C waterlily cutter

Cut 9 small waterlily petals. Colour as before. Push a pinhead down the centre of each petal. Moisten and place before and alternating with the previous row. Repeat with another 9 small waterlily petals.

Cut 9 petals with the T04 petal cutter. Colour, shape and place as before. Repeat with 5 more petals. Allow to dry.

Dust all petals with the same pink, brown and cornflour mixture. Add a touch of silver lustre on the edge of petals, if desired, and brush a little apricot chalk in the centre of the lower petals.

ASSEMBLY

Using stem wrap, tape leaves on to toothpick, cupping around flower.

T04 D cutter

Flame Pea

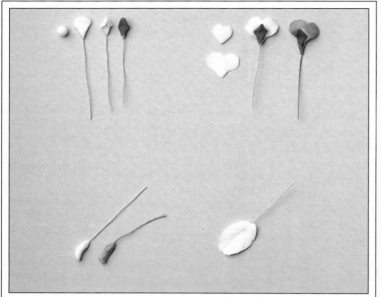

Materials

modelling paste; small pinhead; fine wire; burgundy, lemon yellow, egg yellow, orange, leaf green and caramel brown liquid food colouring; spirits; fine paintbrush; 35b heart cutter; water; royal icing; small rolling pin; scalpel; green parafilm stem wrap

FLOWER
Make *3*

Roll a ball of paste half the size of the small pinhead over hooked wire. Flatten top, then fold sides towards front and tilt top forward. Allow to dry.

Paint with equal parts of burgundy food colouring and spirits. Allow to dry.

Cut a small heart shape. Flute with fingers around top edge to fine petal. Moisten base of petal with equal parts of lemon yellow food colouring and water and place flower centre on it. Turn back petal. Allow to dry.

To colour, paint top and back of petal with a mixture of 3 parts orange and 1 part egg yellow food colouring with 6 parts spirits. Allow to dry. Then paint a 5 star calyx on the base with soft green royal icing.

BUD
Make *2*

Roll small pinheads of paste into shape shown over hooked wire. Mark lengthwise with scalpel, then turn back slightly, making a crescent shape so the scalpel mark is on the outer edge. Allow to dry.

To colour, paint with same orange and yellow mixture as flower, and same calyx.

LEAF
Make *5*

Place a small pinhead of paste over wire. Roll, cut, shape and vein as shown. Using a scalpel, cut small slits on edge of leaf. Allow to dry.

To colour, mix 2 parts leaf green and 1 part caramel brown liquid food colouring with 6 parts spirits.

ASSEMBLY

Twist 3 leaves together. Then, working down the stem, add buds, flowers and more leaves. Secure with stem wrap.

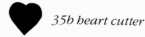 *35b heart cutter*

HAPPY FATHER'S DAY

This simply designed octagonal shaped cake features brightly coloured bottlebrush and the
Kingsmill Mallee Gum.

Pin Cushion Hakea

Materials

*thick tipped and normal stamens; scissors; lemon
yellow, pillar box red, rose pink, sky blue, leaf
green, caramel brown and chocolate brown liquid
food colouring; spirits; modelling paste;
paintbrush; thick and medium wire; royal icing;
size 1 piping tube and bag; pin; tweezers; medium
pinhead; scalpel; cornflour; brush for dusting;
skewer; leaf green and red chalk; brown parafilm
stem wrap*

OPEN FLOWER
Make *1*

Cut the tops off 100 normal stamens, leaving stems
1.5 cm long.

Colour by placing in a mixture of 1 part lemon
yellow liquid food colouring with 20 parts spirits.
Allow to dry.

Roll a ball of paste 2 cm in diameter over hooked
thick wire. Place coloured stamens in the ball 2-3
mm apart, leaving a 2 cm diameter area clear around
the wire to make it easier to assemble flower onto
stem. Allow to dry.

To colour, tint royal icing with equal parts of pillar
box red and rose pink liquid food colouring and,
with the piping tube, pipe dots all over ball of paste
in between the lemon stamen stems.

PARTLY OPEN FLOWER
Make *1*

Cut 50 thick tipped stamens in half, giving 100
pieces.

Using royal icing and piping tube, pipe a hook over
the top of each stamen as shown. Allow to dry. Then
paint each hook very pale yellow, with a mixture of
1 part lemon yellow food colouring and 40 parts
spirits. Cut stamens to 1.5 cm long. Place a small ball
of paste about 1.5 cm in diameter over hooked thick
wire.

Paint a very pale pink with a mixture of 1 part rose
pink and 1 part pillar box red food colouring with
100 parts spirits. Prick all over with a pin.

Using tweezers, place stamens in paste, again leaving
a 1.5 cm diameter area clear around wire.

Pin Cushion Hakea

BUD

Make *1*

Roll a ball of paste the size of the medium pinhead over hooked medium wire to form a cone shape. Mark with scalpel as shown. Allow to dry.

Paint top with a mixture of 1 part caramel brown liquid colouring and 20 parts spirits, and bottom with a mixture of 1 part chocolate brown colouring and 8 parts spirits. Blend the colours together. When dry, dust bud with cornflour and brush off excess.

LEAF

Make 7

Roll paste over a piece of medium wire. Cut, shape and vein with skewer as shown. Dry with a slight curve.

To colour, paint with a mixture of 2 parts leaf green, 1 part caramel brown and a touch of sky blue food colouring and 6 parts spirits. When dry, dust lightly with leaf green chalk and tip the edges with red chalk.

ASSEMBLY

Twist 2 leaves and 1 bud together. Then, working down the stem, add the partly open flower, 3 leaves, then the open flower and finally 2 leaves.

Happy Wanderer

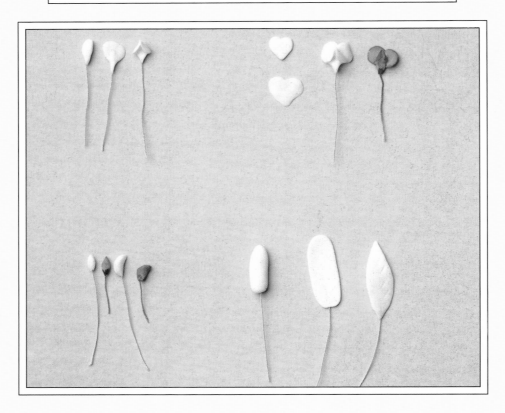

Materials

*modelling paste; small and medium pinheads; fine
wire; small rolling pin; 35b heart cutter; mauve,
rose pink, leaf green, caramel brown and sky blue
liquid food colouring; spirits; fine paintbrush;
scalpel; royal icing; size 0 piping tube and bag;
green parafilm stem wrap*

FLOWER
Make *3*

Mould a ball of paste half the size of the small
pinhead over hooked wire. Roll to shape shown.
Flatten top, then fold in half from the top and tilt top
sides forward to form point at top. Allow to dry. Roll
out modelling paste thinly and cut a small heart
shape. Flute around top edge with fingers to thin
petal. Moisten base of petal and place flower centre
on it. Turn petal back. Allow to dry.

To colour, mix 1 part mauve and 1 part rose pink
liquid food colouring with 25 parts spirits. Allow to
dry, then pipe 2 small green dots of royal icing above
the centre. Paint a small green calyx on base of
flower with undiluted leaf green food colouring.

HALF OPEN FLOWER
Make *2*

Make the same as the flower but wrap petal around
flower centre instead of folding it back.

Paint with mauve and pink mixture, then add green
calyx, as for flower.

SMALL BUD
Make *2*

Mould a ball of paste half the size of the small
pinhead into an oval shape over hooked wire. Allow
to dry.

To colour, paint with mauve and pink mixture. Paint
green calyx on buds.

Happy Wanderer

LEAF

Make *2*

Place a medium pinhead-sized piece of paste over wire. Roll and flatten, cut shape of leaf, vein and allow to dry.

To colour, paint leaves with 2 parts leaf green, 1 part caramel brown and a touch of sky blue liquid food colouring with 10 parts spirits.

MEDIUM BUD

Make *2*

Mould a ball of paste the size of the small pinhead on to an oval shape over hooked wire. Mark one side with scalpel, then turn back slightly into a crescent shape with scalpel mark on outer edge. Allow to dry.

Colour the same as the small bud.

ASSEMBLY

From the top of the stem, start with the small buds, then the medium, the half open flowers, then the flowers and finish with the leaves. Secure with stem wrap as you go.

 35b heart cutter

HAPPY FATHER'S DAY

This simply designed octagonal shaped cake features brightly coloured bottlebrush and the Kingsmill Mallee Gum.

ANNIVERSARY CAKE

First prize Whittlesea Show 1988.

This attractive cake is decorated with a delightful spray of Sturt's Desert Rose, Bladder Pea and Philotheca Salsolifiolia.

Pink Heath

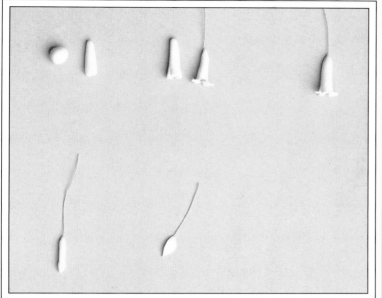

Floral emblem of Victoria

Materials

modelling paste; small pinhead; small rolling pin; fine skewer; scissors; fine wire; small stamens; size 0 piping tube and bag; royal icing; paintbrush; pink chalk; cornflour; brush for dusting; caramel brown, leaf green and sky blue liquid food colouring; spirits

FLOWER
Make 7

Using a ball of paste the size of the small pinhead, roll to shape shown 2 cm long. Insert a fine skewer and hollow slightly.

Make 5 small scissor cuts at the open end to form petals. Shape and flatten them, pointing the ends, and curl back. Insert hooked wire and secure at base of flower. Make 5 small indents with skewer around the base. Insert 5 small stamens keeping close to each petal or pipe 5 small dots of white royal icing just on the inside of each petal. Paint a small 5 star calyx with white royal icing at base (not shown). Allow to dry.

To colour, dust inside and out with 2 parts pink chalk and 1 part cornflour. Paint stamens with a mixture of 1 part caramel brown food colouring and 20 parts spirits.

LEAF
Make 9

Place a ball of paste half the size of the small pinhead over a piece of fine wire. Roll, shape and vein. Allow to dry.

To colour, paint with a mixture of 2 parts leaf green, 1 part caramel brown and a touch of sky blue liquid food colouring with 6 parts spirits.

BUD
Make 5

Make buds of different sizes. Mould small pieces of paste to form shapes 1-2 cm long, with pointed top over hooked wire. Put 5 indents around base with skewer.

Colour the same as the flower.

ASSEMBLY

Start spray with 3 leaves twisted together, then, working down the stem, add buds, flowers and leaves to form a spray.

Kangaroo Paw

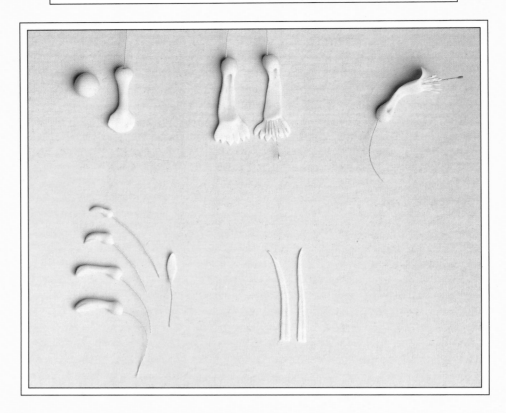

Materials

*modelling paste; leaf green, lemon yellow and
pillar box red liquid food colouring; paintbrush;
small and medium pinheads; fine, medium and
thick wire; small rolling pin; skewer; scissors; fine
stamens; spirits; green and red chalk; brush for
dusting; scalpel; green parafilm stem wrap*

FLOWER
Make *2*

Colour modelling paste leaf green. Place a medium
pinhead sized ball of paste over a piece of hooked
medium wire. Roll between fingers to form a bulb at
base. Flatten top, fanning out slightly.

Roll to flatten centre, forming a slight ridge in which
to place stamens. Make hole in base with skewer. Cut
6 slits in top, shape and vein.

Colour 6 1 cm stamens with 1 part lemon yellow
food colouring diluted with 20 parts spirits, and 1 2
cm stamen with 1 part leaf green food colouring
diluted with 20 parts spirits. Place stamens in ridge.

Bend petals back and dry with a slight curve in
flower as shown.

To colour, paint bulb at base with 1 part pillar box
red and 10 parts spirits. Dust back of flower with
green chalk and red chalk at the base to give a furry
look.

BUD
Make *4*

Mould different sized balls of paste, from medium
pinhead size down to half small pinhead, over fine
hooked wire. Roll between fingers to form bulb at
base. Shape to a point at top making 6 small lines
with scalpel.

To colour, dust all over with green and then red
chalk at the base.

PETAL
Make *6*

Place tiny balls of paste over fine wire 3 cm long.
Roll very thinly and cut a long oval shape. Bend
slightly to dry.

Paint outside of small petals with the pale red mix,
then dust with red chalk, leaving the inside green.

Kangaroo Paw

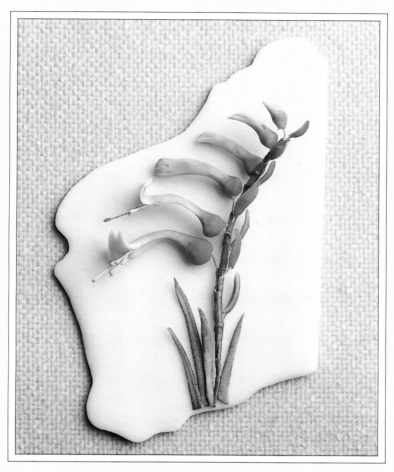

Floral emblem of Western Australia

LEAF

Make 4

The leaves are long and grass-like. Roll paste over fine wire and cut long petals of differing lengths and vein with skewer down the centre. Bend slightly to dry.

To colour, paint with a mixture of 2 parts leaf green and 1 part caramel brown food colouring with 8 parts spirits.

ASSEMBLY

Attach the smallest bud on to a piece of thick wire with stem wrap. Then, working down the stem, add the buds starting with the smallest and finishing with 2 flowers, all on the one side. As you work down the stem add a small petal opposite each of the buds and flowers.

Native Fuchsia

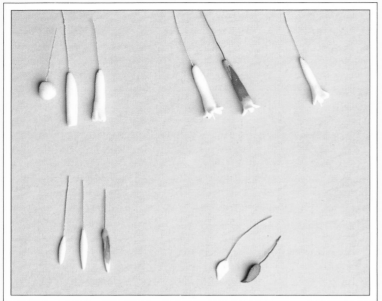

Materials

modelling paste; small and medium pinheads;
fine wire; small rolling pin; skewer; scissors;
stamen stems; rose pink, leaf green and caramel
brown liquid food colouring; fine paintbrush;
royal icing; spirits; green parafilm stem wrap

FLOWER
Make 6

Mould a ball of paste the size of the medium pinhead over hooked wire. Roll to shape shown 2.5 cm long. Push skewer in top to hollow. Make 5 small cuts to form 5 petals.

Flatten and shape each petal to a point. Insert one stamen stem (i.e. top removed) in the centre. Turn petals back slightly.

To make a partly open flower, do the same, but do not turn petals back. Allow to dry.

To colour, paint flower with undiluted rose pink food colouring, leaving petals white. Blend colour between pink and white. Then, with soft royal icing coloured leaf green, paint a 5 star calyx on the base.

BUD
Make 6

Mould a ball of paste the size of the small pinhead into shape shown, pointed at ends over hooked wire. Make various sizes, between 1 and 2 cm long.

To colour, paint bud with undiluted rose pink food colouring, leaving a white top. Paint a calyx as you did for the flower.

LEAF
Make 20

Place a ball of paste half the size of the small pinhead over wire. Roll and shape into a small pointed leaf and vein with skewer. Turn the top back slightly.

To colour, paint with a mixture of 2 parts leaf green and 1 part caramel brown food colouring with 6 parts spirits.

ASSEMBLY

Twist 3 leaves together and secure with stem wrap. Working down, add 4 more leaves. Then add buds and leaves, one at a time alternately, then do the same with the flowers and remaining leaves.

RETIREMENT WISHES

What could be more suitable than a gold watch for a retirement? Decorated with a spray of
Dagger Wattle, Brown Boronia and lime green Correa.

Fuchsia Gum

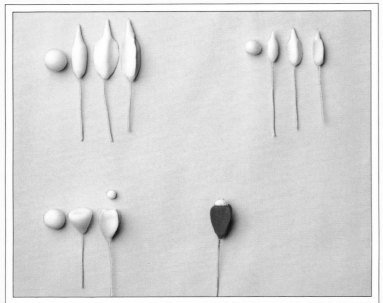

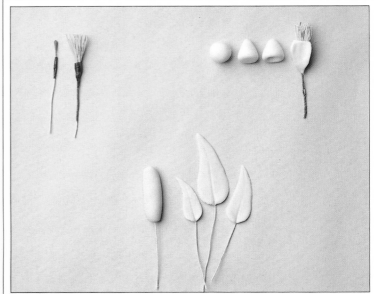

Materials

*white and green modelling paste; small and large
pinheads; medium wire; eggwhite; rose pink, pillar
box red, egg yellow, lemon yellow, leaf green and
caramel brown liquid food colouring; fine
paintbrush; spirits; normal and thick stamens;
scissors; royal icing; brown parafilm stem wrap;
paper towel; small rolling pin; modelling tool or
skewer; T04 A, B and C cutters; lime green,
turquoise and dark orange chalk; brush for dusting*

LARGE BUD
Make 1

Using white modelling paste make a ball the size of
the large pinhead. Hook one end of wire and
moisten it with eggwhite. Insert moistened end
halfway through ball. Roll ball between fingertips
and palm of your hand to make a sausage shape
about 3 cm long. Roll top of sausage again to create
pointed tip. Pinch sides of sausage to flatten them,
wider at the top. Repeat on front and back of shape
to create 4 ridges.

To colour, mix 1 part rose pink and 2 parts pillar box
red liquid food colouring. Paint base of bud. Using 1
part leaf green and 1 part egg yellow food
colouring, paint top of bud. Blend together and
allow to dry.

SMALL BUD
Make 3

Make a ball half the size of the large pinhead and
make as for the large bud, but roll the sausage to
about 2 cm in length.

To colour, mix 1 part lemon yellow and 1 part leaf
green liquid food colouring with 8 parts spirits.
Paint the entire bud.

FLOWERING BUD
Make 1

Hook wire on one end. Using white modelling
paste, mould a cone shape about 2 cm long. Flatten
its top. Moisten hooked end of wire with eggwhite
and insert it halfway through the cone. Push a small
pinhead into the top to make an indentation. Leave
pinhead in cone to ensure shape is not lost. Pinch 4
sides of cone to make 4 ridges, wider at the top. Roll
a ball the size of the small pinhead with white
modelling paste. Moisten centre of cone indentation
with eggwhite and place the ball on it. Insert a
stamen 5 mm long into the ball then take it out.

To colour bud, paint with a mix of 2 parts pillar box
red and 1 part rose pink food colouring with 5 parts
spirits, leaving the ball white, as shown. Allow to
dry. Then pipe fine white lines with royal icing
mixed to firm peak consistency on the ball, replace
stamen and allow to dry.

Fuchsia Gum

To colour ball and stamen, mix 1 part egg yellow liquid food colouring with 5 parts spirits and paint with a fine brush.

FLOWER
Make 2

Colour a thick stamen about 2 cm long with caramel brown before or after taping to wire. Place stamen on top of wire about 4 cm long and wrap together. Snip tops and bottoms off 30 normal stamens and cut to lengths of 2 cm each.

To colour stamens, mix 1 part egg yellow food colouring with 5 parts spirits.

Place the 30 prepared stamens in this mixture. Remove and allow to dry on a paper towel. Place 6 stamens around thick stamen and secure with stem wrap. Continue circling the thick stamen until all the stamens are used. They should sit just a little higher than the centre stamen. Wrap remainder of stem with stem wrap. Roll a ball of white modelling paste the size of the large pinhead. Mould it into a cone shape. Hollow out cone using modelling tool or skewer. Moisten hollowed area with eggwhite and insert prepared stems of stamens. These should protrude over the top of the cone by 1 cm. Pinch base of cone with fingertips to secure stem. Pinch 4 sides of cone to create ridges.

To colour, paint with the same mixture used for the bud.

LEAF
Make *1* large
Make *2* medium
Make *3* small

Roll a thick sausage of green modelling paste about 3 cm long. Moisten one end of wire and insert it halfway through paste. Flatten shape with rolling pin, ensuring wire is in the centre. Using the 3 largest T04 cutters, cut the required number of shapes. Trim with scissors to narrow them. To colour, mix 1 part caramel brown and 2 parts leaf green liquid food colouring with 12 parts spirits to make pale green. Paint all over and allow to dry. To colour small leaves further, dust with lime green chalk. To colour medium and large leaves further, dust with equal parts of lime green and turquoise chalk. Then dust edges and centre veins of all leaves with dark orange chalk.

ASSEMBLY

Make a cluster of 3 small leaves. Below them add 3 small buds and wrap together. Add 2 medium leaves below and to one side of the buds. Further down, add 1 flowering bud, 1 large bud and 1 flower. Place 1 large leaf behind this cluster and wrap together. Wrap 1 more flower just below cluster.

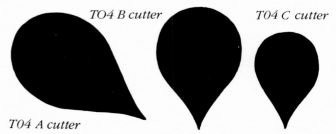

T04 B cutter

T04 C cutter

T04 A cutter

Mallee Gum

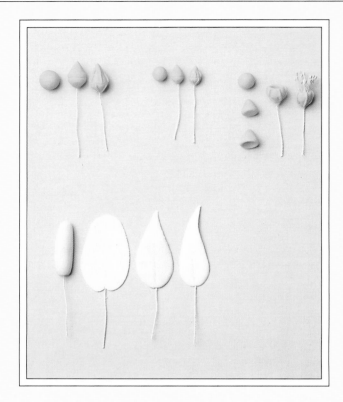

Materials

*red and green modelling paste; medium pinhead;
medium wire; eggwhite; scalpel; tweezers; skewer or
modelling tool; foam; pillar box red, caramel
brown, egg yellow and leaf green liquid food
colouring; spirits; paintbrush; thick and normal
stamens; scissors; paper towel; red royal icing; size
2 piping tube and bag; T04 A cutter; lime green,
khaki and orange chalk; brush for dusting; green
parafilm stem wrap*

LARGE BUD
Make 3

Roll a ball of red modelling paste the size of the large
pinhead. Hook one end of wire. Moisten with
eggwhite and insert halfway through ball. Mould
ball into tear shape and make a point at the top.
Using the scalpel, etch a line around the middle of
tear shape. Pinch 6 ridges around the sides of the
bottom half with the tweezers. Repeat on the top
half placing ridges between lower ridges. Allow to
dry.

SMALL BUD
Make 3

Roll a ball half the size of the large pinhead and do
the same as for the large bud.

FLOWER
Make 3

Roll a ball of red modelling paste half the size of the
large pinhead and mould it into a cone shape.
Flatten the top. Using a skewer or modelling tool,
hollow its centre. Hook one end of wire. Moisten
hook with eggwhite and insert it through the centre
of the cone. Secure by pinching base of cone. Insert
the medium pinhead into hollow of cone and rotate
on foam to form cup shape. With the pinhead still in
the cone, to ensure the cone does not lose its shape,
turn it upside down and pinch the sides with
tweezers to make 6 ridges. Remove the pinhead and
pinch the top of each ridge. This slightly closes the
cone and also makes the ridge more prominent.
Allow to dry.

To colour buds and flowers, mix 1 part pillar box red
and 1 part caramel brown food colouring with 6
parts spirits and paint the buds all over and the base
of the flowers.

Mallee Gum

To prepare flower centre, cut an entire packet of normal stamens 1 cm long, leaving the tips on. Place them in a mixture of 1 part egg yellow food colouring with 12 parts spirits. Allow to dry on a paper towel. Fill hollow of cone with royal icing of medium peak consistency. Insert a thick stamen into the centre. Using tweezers insert 20 stamens around it. Allow to dry.

LEAF
Make 5

Cut a leaf from the green modelling paste, using the cutter. Trim to a narrower shape, as shown, with the scissors.

To colour leaves, mix 1 part caramel brown and 2 parts leaf green food colouring with 10 parts spirits. Paint all over and allow to dry. Then, dust all over with equal parts of lime green and khaki chalk. Dust outer edges and vein with orange chalk.

ASSEMBLY

Assemble 3 separate sprays. For the first, simply tape 3 small buds together. For the second, tape 2 large buds and 1 flower together. For the third, tape 1 large bud and 2 flowers together. Then place the base of one leaf about 1 cm below the first spray and secure. Working down the stem, place a leaf on either side. Place the second spray on the right side just below these leaves, then place the remaining spray about 1 cm below this. Attach 1 leaf on the right and cover remainder of stem with stem wrap.

T04 A cutter

Kingsmill Mallee

Materials

white modelling paste; medium pinhead; medium wire; eggwhite; scalpel; tweezers; skewer or modelling tool; foam; caramel brown, egg yellow and leaf green liquid food colouring; spirits; paintbrush; thick and normal stamens; scissors; paper towel; pale yellow royal icing; size 2 piping tube and bag; T04 A cutter; brown, lime green and yellow chalk; brush for dusting; green parafilm stem wrap

T04 A cutter

This is made in substantially the same way, but with the following differences.

Use white modelling paste for the buds and flowers.

Stamens are coloured with a mixture of 1 part egg yellow food colouring and 30 parts spirits.

The leaf shape is slender, not broad. Therefore trim cut shape even more.

Paint small buds with a mixture of 1 part egg yellow and 1 part leaf green food colouring with 40 parts spirits.

Paint the large buds and flower bases with 1 part egg yellow and 60 parts spirits. When assembling flower, fill hollow cone with pale yellow, not red, royal icing.

For the leaves, paint all over with a mixture of 1 part caramel brown and 2 parts leaf green food colouring with 10 parts spirits. Then dust with a mixture of 1 part brown and 2 parts lime green chalk. Finally, dust outer edges and vein with yellow chalk.

AUSTRALIAN CHRISTMAS CAKE
First prize Royal Melbourne Show 1988.
Sprays of Robyn Gordon Grevillea and Pin Cushion Hakea adorn this cake which also won a
special award from the Australian Natives Association at the 1988 Royal Melbourne Show.

Coral Candy Tea Tree

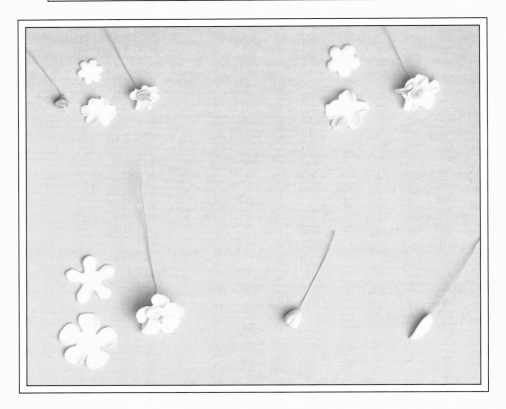

Materials

modelling paste; small pinhead; fine wire; stamens; scissors; rolling pin; 7010 lily of the valley, 7902 small blossom and 8201 blossom cutters; toothpick; skewer; paintbrush; royal icing; pink chalk; cornflour; brush for dusting; rose pink, caramel brown and leaf green liquid food colouring; spirits; scalpel; green parafilm stem wrap

FLOWER
Make 3

Attach a ball of leaf green paste half the size of the small pinhead over hooked wire. Flatten top and place a 5 mm length of stamen in the centre. Allow to dry.

Roll out modelling paste and cut 1 lily of the valley shape and flute edge with a toothpick or skewer. Moisten and cup around centre ball.

Cut 1 small blossom shape and flute edge with toothpick. Moisten and place around first petal.

Cut 1 blossom shape. Flute petals with toothpick to thin out edges. Moisten and attach to flower. Insert 5

5 mm stamens around centre. Paint a 5 star calyx on back of flower with leaf green royal icing.

To colour, dust flower with a mixture of 4 parts pink chalk and 1 part cornflour to give a variegated effect. Paint the centre dark pink with a mixture of equal parts of rose pink and caramel brown food colouring and of spirits.

BUD
Make 3

Attach small balls of paste, varying in size from the small to the medium pinhead, over a 4 cm length of hooked wire. Shape and make 5 indents in top with scalpel. Paint a 5 star calyx with leaf green royal icing around the base (not shown).

Coral Candy Tea Tree

LEAF
Make 9

Place a small ball of paste half the size of the small pinhead over a piece of wire and roll to a thin cylindrical shape. Flatten and vein. Allow to dry.

To colour, paint with 2 parts leaf green and 1 part caramel brown liquid colouring with 6 parts spirits.

ASSEMBLY

Twist 3 leaves together at the top with stem wrap. Working down the stem add 2 more leaves and 2 buds. Add 3 flowers, at different levels, then 2 leaves, finishing off with a bud and another 2 leaves.

 7010 lily of the valley cutter

 8201 blossom cutter

 7902 small blossom cutter

Sturt's Desert Rose

Materials

*modelling paste; royal icing; fine and medium
wire; black, maroon, pink and mauve chalk;
cornflour; T04 B and C cutters; pin; tin foil;
airtight container; satay stick; 8202 hyacinth
cutter; 8306 border cutters; leaf green, lemon
yellow and caramel brown liquid food colouring;
spirits*

FLOWER
Make 2

Roll a ball of pale yellow modelling paste slightly
larger than the medium pinhead. Roll between
fingers and shape as shown on medium wire. Allow
to dry. Then with firm peak consistency white royal
icing dot the base as shown and allow to dry.

To colour, dust base with a mixture of 1 part black
and 2 parts maroon chalk.

Take a 7.5cm square of foil and pleat with fingers in
several places to make a cone shape. Make a hole in
the centre. Roll out modelling paste and cut 5 petals
with the T04 B petal cutter. Place them in container.
Take 1 petal at a time and flute sides and top with
satay stick. Insert fine wire into base of petals, place
in foil cone to shape them and then place centre of
flower inside. Do the same with the other petals,
arranging them around centre. Allow to dry. Remove
from foil.

To colour, dust with a mixture of 1 part each of

mauve and pink chalk and 4 parts cornflour. Then
dust the inner base with maroon mixture and
rearrange petals around centre. For the calyx, cut a
shape with the hyacinth cutter from modelling paste
coloured green. Roll satay stick over each petal to
vein it. Then moisten calyx with eggwhite to secure
it around base of flower.

CENTRE OF BUD
Make 1

Make a small hook on one end of medium wire.
Moisten hook with eggwhite. Roll a ball of white
modelling paste slightly larger than the medium
pinhead and insert moistened wire halfway. Shape
as shown. Allow to dry.

Dust with maroon chalk.

8306 border cutters

Sturt's Desert Rose

Floral emblem of the Northern Territory

BUD
Make *1*

Roll out modelling paste finely, cut 5 petals with the T04 C petal cutter and place in container. Take 1 petal at a time and flute on top with satay stick. Then moisten base of petals with eggwhite and overlap as shown.

To colour, dust base of petals with maroon and black chalk mixture. Roll petals around centre bud. Allow to dry. Dust bud with pink and mauve mixture. Place calyx on base of bud in the same way as for the flower.

LEAF
Make *1* medium
Make *3* large

Roll out sausage shape on fine wire of leaf green modelling paste until thin. Cut leaves using the two larger border cutters. Flatten the edges of each leaf with your fingertips. Using a pin, etch veins on the leaf as shown. Allow to dry.

To colour, mix 1 part leaf green, 1 part lemon yellow and 1 part caramel brown with 25 parts spirits. Paint leaves with the mixture.

ASSEMBLY

Working down the stem, start with the bud, then add 1 flower. Place 1 large and 1 medium leaf on one side of the flower and another large leaf on the other side. Then, further down, add the second flower and remaining leaf.

TO4 B cutter   T04 C cutter   *8202 hyacinth cutter*

Dagger Wattle

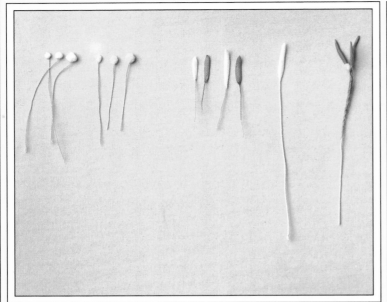

Materials

*royal icing; size 1 piping tube and bag; fine and
medium wire; lemon yellow, leaf green and
caramel brown liquid food colouring; water;
paintbrush; castor sugar; spirits; modelling paste;
green parafilm stem wrap*

FLOWER
Make *42*

Pipe small balls of icing of different sizes on top of
fine wire. Allow to dry.

Colour the balls with 1 part pale lemon yellow food
colouring and 10 parts water, then roll in castor
sugar.

LEAF
Make *51*

Roll a small ball of paste about half the size of the

small pinhead over a piece of fine wire. Mould to a
long narrow shape, flatten and curve slightly. Allow
to dry. Vary leaf size between 1 and 2 cm.

To colour, paint with 2 parts leaf green and 1 part
caramel brown food colouring with 10 parts spirits.

ASSEMBLY

Mould a small leaf on top of a 12 cm length of
medium wire. Secure 2 or 3 leaves at the top of the
stem with one small flower. Working down the stem
add 1 leaf and 1 flower increasing the sizes of leaves
and flowers as you go. Make 3 stems and secure with
stem wrap.

CHRISTMAS BELL

Different shades of Rosemary Grevillea decorate this bell-shaped Christmas cake.

Cat's Paw

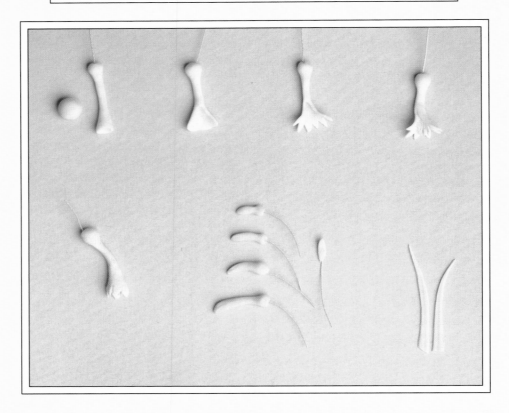

Materials

modelling paste; leaf green, egg yellow, pillar box red, caramel brown and rose pink liquid food colouring; medium paintbrush; spirits; small rolling pin; medium pinhead; fine, medium and thick wire; skewer; scissors; tweezers; stamens; scalpel; pink and brown chalk; brush for dusting; brown parafilm stem wrap

FLOWER
Make 3

Colour 6 stamen tips with 1 part egg yellow food colouring to 20 parts spirits. Colour modelling paste pale leaf green.

Roll a medium pinhead sized ball of paste over a piece of hooked medium wire. Roll between fingers to form bulb at base. With skewer or modelling tool, hollow out top.

Cut a slit 1.5 cm in it and fan out. Cut a further 6 slits in the top, shape each piece to make petals pointed and vein inside each one with a skewer. Insert, using tweezers, yellow tipped stamens 7 mm long and turn petals slightly back. Dry with a slight bend.

HALF OPEN FLOWER
Make 5

Make as above, but after inserting the stamens, curl petals inwards.

BUD
Make 8

Roll small balls of paste ranging in size from the small to the medium pinhead, over hooked fine wire. Roll between fingers to form bulb at base. Point top end, etching 6 small lines with scalpel. Slightly bend to dry.

To colour flower and bud, paint bulb at base with a very pale mixture of 1 part pillar box red and 1 part rose pink food colouring with 20 parts spirits. Then dust over the outside with a mixture of 3 parts pink and 1 part brown chalk, leaving the inside green.

Cat's Paw

PETAL
Make *16*

Place a tiny ball of paste over fine wire 3 cm long. Roll until very thin, and cut 1 tiny oval petal. Bend slightly. Make one for each bud and flower.

To colour, dust over the outside with a mixture of 3 parts pink and 1 part brown chalk, leaving the inside green.

LEAF
Make *4*

The leaves are long and grass-like. Roll paste over fine wire and cut long leaves of differing lengths, 3-4 cm long. Vein down the centre with skewer and bend slightly to dry.

To colour, paint with a mixture of 2 parts leaf green and 1 part caramel brown liquid food colouring with 8 parts spirits.

ASSEMBLY

Attach the smallest bud on to a piece of thick wire with stem wrap and then add remaining buds and flowers around the wire, always attaching a petal opposite each bud and flower.

Astartea Fascicularis

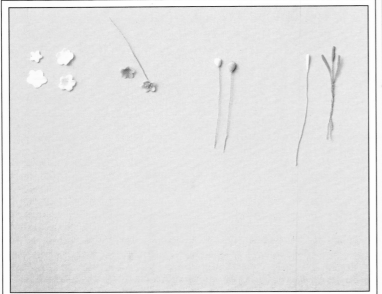

Materials

modelling paste; rolling pin; 7903 forget-me-not cutter; toothpick; foam; small pinhead; pink chalk; cornflour; brush for dusting; fine wire; royal icing; size 0 piping tube and bag; scissors; leaf green and caramel brown liquid food colouring; spirits; small paintbrush; green parafilm stem wrap

FLOWER
Make 5

Roll paste thinly and cut out shapes with forget-me-not cutter. Roll each petal with toothpick to widen. Turn flower over on to foam and press pinhead into each petal. Turn flower over and press pinhead into centre. Make a small hole in centre to put wire through when dry. Allow to dry.

Dust centre with a mixture of 2 parts pink chalk and 1 part cornflour. Put a 4 cm length of hooked wire through the small hole. Fill centre of flower with flooding consistency royal icing coloured leaf green, pulling wire down into the icing. Paint a calyx on back of flower with green royal icing. When dry, pipe a row of small pink dots around the green centre.

BUD
Make 5

Mould balls of paste the size of the small pinhead over a length of hooked wire. Dust top with pink chalk. Paint a calyx on with leaf green royal icing.

LEAF
Make 9

Dip a 4 cm length of wire into flooding consistency white royal icing, to form a very narrow leaf about 1 cm long.

When dry, paint with a mixture of 2 parts leaf green and 1 part caramel brown liquid food colouring with 12 parts spirits.

ASSEMBLY

Start spray with 5 leaves taped together. Then, working down the stem, add buds and flowers interspersed with leaves.

 7903 forget-me-not cutter

A spray of flowering gum sets off the spinning wheel. A basket of Flame Pea sits beside the artists easel.

The arrangement in the hessian bag is a mixture of Golden Everlasting flowering gum, Flame Pea and Dagger Wattle.

Robyn Gordon Grevillea

Materials

royal icing; size 1 piping tube and bag; waxed paper; fine and medium wire; small scissors; leaf green, caramel brown and pillar box red liquid food colouring; spirits; fine paintbrush; pale grey and red chalk; brush for dusting; modelling paste; rolling pin; skewer; green parafilm stem wrap

SMALL FLOWER
Make *9*

Pipe 9 pairs of grevillea on to waxed paper with royal icing at soft peak consistency. Allow to dry.

Join pairs together with firm royal icing, with a 4 cm length of hooked fine wire in between.

To colour, paint with a mixture of 1 part leaf green and 1 part caramel brown food colouring with 150 parts spirits. When dry, dust with pale green chalk.

MEDIUM FLOWER
Make *10*

Pipe 10 pairs of grevillea on to waxed paper. Allow to dry. Join pairs together as before with a 5 cm length of hooked fine wire in between.

To colour, paint the top half with 1 part pillar box red diluted with 70 parts spirits, and the bottom half with a mixture 1 part leaf green and 1 part caramel brown food colouring with 150 parts spirits. When dry, dust with pale grey chalk.

LARGE FLOWER
Make *10*

Pipe 10 pairs of grevillea on to waxed paper. Allow to dry. Join pairs together as before with a 5 cm length of hooked fine wire.

To colour, paint the top half with 1 part pillar box red diluted with 50 parts spirits and the bottom half with 1 part leaf green and 1 part caramel brown food colouring with 150 parts spirits. When dry, dust with pale grey chalk.

OPEN FLOWER
Make *12*

Pipe 12 pairs of grevillea on to waxed paper. Allow to dry. Cut 12 pieces of fine wire 8 cm long. Dip one end in very soft royal icing to form a small dot. Allow to dry.

Join pairs together with royal icing with the wire protruding 2.5 cm above top of flower.

Robyn Gordon Grevillea

Pinch halves at centre back, slightly separating pairs, to open flower. Fill bottom opening with firm royal icing to form a bulb. Tidy up and round off bulb with a paintbrush.

To colour, paint the top half with 1 part pillar box red food colouring diluted with 20 parts spirits and the bottom half with 1 part pillar box red diluted with 50 parts spirits. When dry, dust with red chalk.

small flower

large flower

medium flower

open flower

LEAF

Make 5

Place a ball of modelling paste over a 5 cm length of fine wire. Roll and flatten, then cut, shape and vein as shown, making 1 large, 2 medium and 2 small leaves. Secure leaves together as shown.

To colour, paint with a mixture of 1 part caramel brown and 2 parts leaf green liquid food colouring with 10 parts spirits.

ASSEMBLY

Bind 1 small flower on to a length of medium wire using stem wrap, then add two more below it. Use all of the small flowers, gradually making the spray wider as you work down the stem using medium flowers then large and finally the open flowers. Add leaves to finish spray.

Flannel Flower

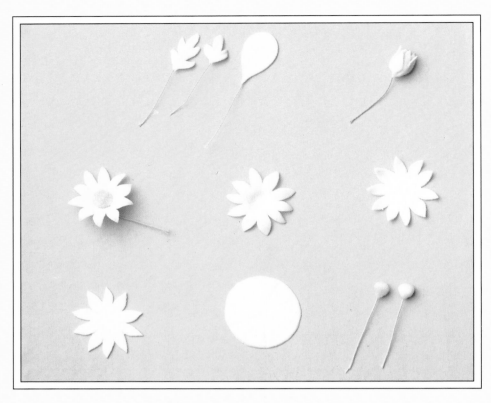

Materials

*modelling paste; small and medium pinheads; fine
and medium wire; leaf green and caramel brown
liquid food colouring; water; fine paintbrush;
castor sugar; 3.5 cm round cutter; skewer; foam;
eggwhite; off-white chalk; brush for dusting; small
rolling pin; T04 petal cutters; spirits*

FLOWER
Make 3

Colour modelling paste leaf green. Mould a ball of
paste the size of the medium pinhead over a piece of
medium hooked wire. Allow to dry.

To colour, paint with a mixture of very pale leaf
green and caramel brown food colouring and a lot
of water. Roll top half of ball in castor sugar.

Cut a circle from modelling paste 3.5 cm in
diameter. Divide into 10 equal parts with skewer.
Using skewer marks as a guide, cut out 10 petals
with scissors. Turn flower over on to foam. Push
back of each petal into foam with the small pinhead
to curl up. Turn over again and push centre into
foam with the medium pinhead to make indent in
centre. Pull wire through and attach sugared ball to
centre of petals with a little water or eggwhite.
Allow to dry.

To colour, paint tips of petals with pale green — 1
part leaf green food colouring with 50 parts spirits.
Then dust petals with off-white chalk to give a soft,
furry effect.

BUD
Make 2

Make as for flower but enclose sugared ball with
petals.

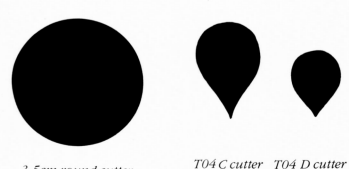

3.5cm round cutter   T04 C cutter   T04 D cutter

Flannel Flower

LEAF

Make 5

Place a small pinhead sized ball of paste over fine wire. Roll paste, cut 3 small and 2 large shapes with petal cutters, then cut to shapes shown. Vein and allow to dry.

To colour, paint with a mixture of 2 parts leaf green and 1 part caramel brown food colouring with 10 parts spirits.

ASSEMBLY

Start with flowers and buds at the top and add leaves at the base of the spray.

BIRDS' NEST

Second prize Royal Melbourne Show 1988.
This plaque features the popular Happy Wanderer.

TABLE SETTING

This flower arrangement makes an ideal novelty table setting. It features gum leaf name tags,
a serviette with gumnuts and wattle and a bowl of Golden Everlasting, wattle and gumnuts.

These delightful koalas make a cute pair among Eucalyptus Blue Gum and Waratah.

Many native flowers are popular for making wreaths. The combination we have chosen is
Kingsmill Mallee Gum, Brown Boronia and wattle.

Sturt's Desert Pea

Materials

fine and medium wire; eggwhite; rolling pin; red and green modelling paste; T04 petal cutters; satay stick; pillar box red and black liquid food colouring; medium paintbrush; scalpel; medium pinhead; foam; small pin; green chalk; brush for dusting; 7082 small hyacinth cutter; green parafilm stem wrap; arabic gum; rose water; small airtight container

BUD
Make 4

Roll out red modelling paste. Using the medium wire make a small hook on one end. Moisten hook with eggwhite. Using the second smallest T04 petal cutter, cut one shape. Roll into a small ball and insert moistened wire halfway. Shape with fingertips into a half circle.

Using the size T04 C cutter, cut a shape. Roll out from the centre with a satay stick to vein and flatten. Leave the veined side on the outside; moisten the inside edge with eggwhite and wrap petal over bud. Press outer edges together to seal. Three of the buds are used in making the flowers.

Paint with undiluted pillar box red colouring. Allow to dry.

FLOWER
Make 3

Cut a shape using the second smallest T04 cutter. Using the satay stick, roll out from the centre, to flatten and vein. Using the scalpel, make an incision three-quarters of the way down the petal. With the veined side on top, slightly part the cut petal to either side. Moisten the bottom of the underside with eggwhite. Place on top of bud and secure by pressing with fingertips.

Cut one shape using the second largest T04 cutter. Roll out as before with the satay stick. Fold petal in half with the vein inside, to achieve the centre vein. Unfold. Place the petal vein side down on foam. Press the medium pinhead either side of the vein near the base. Turn over, and you will have 2 bulges protruding from the petal. Moisten the base of the petal, below the bulges, with eggwhite. Place the petal on front of bud and secure base around stem. Hold secured base in fingertips and gently pull petal away from bud. Allow to dry. Paint entire flower with pillar box red. Allow to dry. Paint the 2 bulges with black liquid colouring.

CALYX
Make 4

Cut 1 shape with the hyacinth cutter. Roll satay stick over each individual petal to vein and slightly flatten. The veined side is the outside. Moisten the underside with eggwhite, and thread on to stem. Secure around base of flower or bud.

Sturt's Desert Pea

Floral emblem of South Australia

LEAF
Make 6

Make a small pea-sized ball. Roll into a fat sausage. Insert moistened end of fine wire halfway. Flatten with a rolling pin. Cut with smallest T04 cutter. Vein down the centre using a small pin. Slightly fold sides of leaf inwards. Allow to dry. Dust with green chalk.

ASSEMBLY

Position 3 flowers and 1 bud in a cluster. Three-quarters of the way down the flower stems, join with stem wrap. Arrange flowers facing outwards. To assemble the leaves, you will need a 12 cm length of medium wire. Start covering the top of the wire with stem wrap. As you move down the wire, attach individual leaves. After attaching 5 or 6 leaves attach remainder of medium wire to the base of the flower stems. Remember, this is a runner and should not be clustered too close together. To make the black 'eyes' of the flower shiny, paint arabic gum mixture on to the dried black paint. To make this, mix 1 part arabic gum with 1 part rose water and let it stand for two days in a small airtight container.

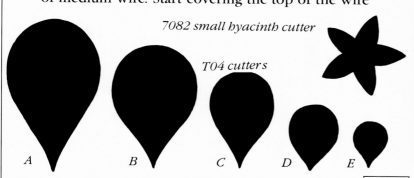

7082 small hyacinth cutter

T04 cutters

A   B   C   D   E

Geraldton Wax

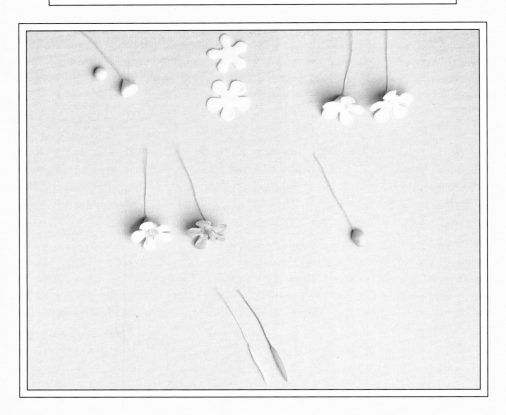

Materials

*modelling paste; small and medium pinheads;
fine wire; scissors; royal icing; rolling pin; 8201
blossom cutter; toothpick; small tipped stamens;
caramel brown and leaf green liquid food
colouring; paintbrush; pink and mauve chalk;
cornflour; brush for dusting; spirits; green
parafilm stem wrap*

FLOWER
Make 7

To make the centre, mould a ball of paste the size of
the medium pinhead over a length of hooked wire.
Push a small pinhead in the top to hollow out.

Roll modelling paste fairly thinly. Cut out shape
with blossom cutter. Roll each petal from side with
toothpick to widen slightly.

Moisten back of flower and place on top of centre.
Push in gently with the small pinhead. Place a row
of 7 stamens 5 cm long around the centre and one
stamen slightly longer in the middle. Allow to dry.

Fill the centre with flooding consistency royal icing,
coloured leaf green.

When dry, paint the centre with a mixture of 1 part
caramel brown food colouring with 30 parts spirits.

Then tip stamens with a touch of this mixture.
When flower is dry, dust edges of petals with a
mixture of 4 parts pink and 1 part mauve chalk with
2 parts cornflour. Paint on a cup shaped calyx with
leaf green royal icing.

BUD
Make 5

Mould small balls of paste, 2 half the size of the small
pinhead and 3 the size of the small pinhead, over 4
cm lengths of hooked wire.

When dry, dust with the pink and mauve chalk
mixture. Paint on a calyx with leaf green royal icing.

Geraldton Wax

LEAF
Make 9

Mould small balls of paste half the size of the small pinhead over the top of wire. Roll to form very fine needle-like leaves, 2 cm long.

To colour, paint with a mixture of 2 parts leaf green and 1 part caramel brown liquid food colouring with 10 parts spirits.

 8201 blossom cutter

ASSEMBLY

Twist together 5 leaves and 2 buds at the top of your spray, then work downwards adding flowers, buds and leaves, securing then with stem wrap as you go.

Bladder Pea

Materials

modelling paste; fine and medium wire; eggwhite;
8202 hyacinth cutter; satay stick; scissors; leaf green
and egg yellow liquid food colouring; spirits; T04 E
petal cutter; T12 E petal cutter; yellow chalk; green
parafilm stem wrap

CALYX

Make *2* open
Make *1* closed

Roll a ball of modelling paste the size of the medium pinhead. Make a small hook on one end of medium wire. Moisten it with eggwhite and insert halfway into ball. Shape with fingertips as shown. Allow to dry.

Cut two shapes with the hyacinth cutter. Roll satay stick over the bottom two petals and cut one third off the bottom edge of the two side petals. Moisten the back of the two bottom petals and wrap over bud. Press outer edges together to seal. Make an open calyx by turning the top petal slightly back and the side petals slightly forward. Make a half closed calyx by turning the top and side petals foward. Allow to dry.

To colour, paint with 1 part leaf green food colouring and 20 parts spirits. Allow to dry.

FLOWER

Make *3*

Cut one shape with the T04 E cutter. Flute with satay stick at the same time you are veining the petals. Cut a 'V' with scissors and fold petal in half, with the veining inside, to form the centre vein. Unfold and moisten base of petal with eggwhite vein side up. Place on bottom of calyx. This is the first of the two petals which form this flower.

Cut one shape with the T12 E petal cutter. Flute with satay stick, at the same time you are veining this second petal. Cut a 'V' out of the top and cut off the point of the base. Fold petal in half as before. Unfold, moisten base of petal with eggwhite vein side up. Place petal face down, secure the base and turn it back on the calyx. Use the same method for the open as for the half closed calyx. Allow to dry.

Colour the centre with yellow chalk.

Bladder Pea

BUD
Make 6

Roll a small ball of modelling paste slightly larger than the medium pinhead. Insert moistened medium wire half way into ball. Shape as shown veining side with pin. Allow to dry.

Dust buds with yellow chalk.

LEAF
Make 15

Take a ball of modelling paste the size of the medium pinhead and roll it into a thin cylindrical shape. Moisten one end of fine wire with eggwhite. Insert wire into paste and roll between two fingers and the palm of your hand. Nip off the top and bottom and roll again to thin out the paste. Repeat until you have a thin leaf about 1 cm long. Allow to dry.

To colour, paint with a mixture of 2 parts leaf green and 1 part egg yellow liquid food colouring with 30 parts spirits.

ASSEMBLY

Make 3 sprays. For the first, secure 3 buds with green parafilm stem wrap. Then secure 5 leaves and 1 open flower below them. For the second, secure 5 leaves and 1 half closed flower together. Secure to the side of the first spray. For the third, secure another 3 buds together. Add this spray to the other with stem wrap. Add 5 leaves and 1 more open flower and stem wrap down the remaining stem.

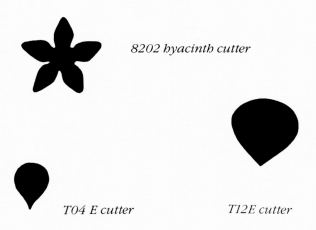

8202 hyacinth cutter

T04 E cutter

T12E cutter

List of Suppliers

NEW SOUTH WALES

CAKE DECORATORS SUPPLIES
770 George Street
SYDNEY NSW 2000

EDIBLE ART SUPPLIES
Mail Order Service
Pultney Arcade
TAREE NSW 2430

*CANDYMAN CAKE DECORATING
EQUIPMENT*
7 Parkes Street
MANLY VALE NSW 2093

VICTORIA

SUSIE-Q CAKE DECORATING CENTRE
372 Keilor Road
NIDDRIE VIC 3042   or

1137 Toorak Road
HARTWELL VIC 3124

QUEENSLAND

CAKE ICING CENTRE
651 Samford Road
MITCHELTON QLD 4053

CAKE ORNAMENT CO.
156 Alfred Street
FORTITUDE VALLEY QLD 4006

PROSERPINE CAKE DECORATING SUPPLIES
24A Chapman Street
PROSERPINE QLD 4800

THE ICING PLACE
6 Wighton Street
MARGATE QLD 4019

SOUTH AUSTRALIA

CAKE DECORATING CENTRE
7 Adelaide Arcade
ADELAIDE SA 5000

WESTERN AUSTRALIA

CAKE DECORATORS SHOP
Shop 2/4b Webber Street
WILLAGEE WA 6156

MIDLAND CAKE DECORATION CENTRE
11 The Avenue
MIDLAND WA 6056

PETERSEN'S CAKE DECORATIONS
Rear 698 Beaufort Street
MOUNT LAWLEY WA 6050

TASMANIA

CORYULE CAKE DECORATING
31 Cambridge Road
BELLERIVE TAS 7018

Page Index for Flowers